AUSTERITY

The DEMOLITION of the WELFARE STATE and the RISE of the ZOMBIE ECONOMY

KERRY-ANNE MENDOZA

Contents

Introduction..7

PART ONE: THE DEMOLITION

1 The road to Austerity..10

2 The rise of the zombie economy..21

3 The destruction of the NHS 28

4 Privatizing education 43

5 The assault on social security..54

6 Austerity in Britain: some conclusions....................................78

PART TWO: AUSTERITY AND DEMOCRACY

7 Creating the culture that invites Austerity............................86

8 The rise of corporate fascism... 106

9 Attacking employment rights 121

10 Outsourcing the justice system 134

11 Civil liberties, human rights and democracy.................... 146

12 The endgame of Austerity...171

About the author

Kerry-anne Mendoza is a writer, blogger and activist. She is the author of the Scriptonite Daily blog, which explores matters of current affairs, politics, economics and ideas. She is also a contributor to *New Internationalist, openDemocracy, Trebuchet Magazine*, the *Occupy News Network* and others.

She left her career as a management consultant, having held senior positions in banking, local government and the NHS, to be part of the Occupy Movement and has since worked as a writer and campaigner for social, economic and environmental justice.

Introduction

In July 1944, the soon-to-be victorious powers of the Second World War met in Bretton Woods, New Hampshire. Their mission: to lay down the architecture of the post-War global political and economic systems. They stated that their aim was to free the world from fascism forever. In reality, they built the foundations for a new fascism – corporate fascism – and modern Austerity is merely a vehicle to deliver it.

Austerity is not a short-term disruption to balance the books. It is the demolition of the welfare state – transferring the UK from social democracy to corporate power. We are witnessing the end and not the beginning of a process, set in train at the close of the Second World War, at Bretton Woods.

Austerity has been presented as necessary, constructive and temporary by governments across the world, the UK included. By the end of this book, it will be clear to the reader that Austerity is unnecessary, destructive and intended as a permanent break with the traditions of social democracy.

This book explores the methods by which the pillars of social democracy – law and justice, employment rights, civil liberties and human rights, and the welfare state – have been bulldozed, one after the other, under the guise of Austerity.

This destruction has happened so cynically and quickly in Britain that, without having kept a constant eye on the issues at hand, many people still believe they live in a social democracy and that they hold rights that were confiscated long ago. Sadly, they will not realize that those once-cherished rights are now defunct until they try, for the first time in their lives, to claim them.

Kerry-anne Mendoza

PART ONE: THE DEMOLITION

1
The road to Austerity

The birth of the neoliberal project

AUSTERITY did not start in the UK in 2010 or Greece in 2009. It has been a tactic used to deliver the goals of the neoliberal project throughout the latter half of the 20th century. Most of the economic policies and institutions delivering Austerity today were set up in the final months of the Second World War.

In 1944, before the end of World War Two, a conference took place in Bretton Woods, New Hampshire. It was at this conference that the US, now with the world's largest standing army and the only functioning economy in the West, set out the framework for the neoliberal project. The International Monetary and Financial Conference of the United and Associated Nations[1] was led by US Secretary of the Treasury Henry Morgenthau, his chief economic advisor Harry Dexter White, and leading British economist John Maynard Keynes – although Keynes and White had been working on plans for post-War economic co-operation since at least 1941.[2] The conference took place at the Mount Washington Hotel in Bretton Woods, from 1 to 22 July 1944. Delegations from 44 nations attended, including a 30-member delegation from China (second only to the US in size), and no fewer than seven future prime ministers and presidents.

The representatives were keen to establish a stable post-War economy, concerned to avoid the economic warfare, hyper-inflation and market instabilities of the inter-war period. But there were other motives. The major colonial powers of Europe –

Austria, Hungary, the UK, France and Germany – were stricken. Their economies were no longer fully functioning and each country had sustained enormous damage to its infrastructure. What would become of the colonies, and their supply of free or cheap labour and natural resources to the Great Powers? These questions were of great importance to the delegates at Bretton Woods. As in 1884, when the colonial powers had met at the Berlin Conference to carve up between them what King Leopold of Belgium described as 'this magnificent African cake' – so too, the powers of 1944 were motivated by empire, albeit a transformed version of the idea.

Unlike in 1884, there was a new and powerful negotiator at the table: the United States of America.

An insight into the thinking of Britain at this time comes from a speech Winston Churchill made to Parliament on 'Empire and Commonwealth Unity' on 21 April 1944.

'A great number of these questions concern our future, and they have been raised directly or indirectly. What changes are to be made in the political, economic and defence structure of the British Commonwealth and Empire? In what way will an ever more closely knitted British Commonwealth and Empire become also, at the same time, more closely associated with the United States? How will this vast bloc of States and Nations, which will walk along together, speaking, to a large extent, the same language, reposing on the same body of common law, be merged in the supreme council for the maintenance of world peace? Should we draw closer to Europe – there is another question – and aim at creating, under the Supreme World Council, a living union, an entity in Europe, a United States of Europe? Or, again, should we concentrate upon our own Imperial and Commonwealth organization, or upon our fraternal association with the United States, and put our trust in the English Channel, in air power, and in sea power?

'Other more familiar topics than these – because it is easy to see, from the recurrence of these topics in so many speeches, the way in which the modern mind of the House is moving –

have been raised, like Free Trade versus Protection, Imperial Preference versus greater development of international trade, and international currency in relation to the policy of the United States and the existence of a vast sterling area. One even sees the gold standard peering around the corner, and, of course, British agriculture close at hand.'[3]

This section of the speech captures the dilemmas Churchill was wrestling with: the real need for US financial and political support; the question (which remains today) of whether to ally primarily with Europe or the US; and the fate of the British Empire. Churchill refers to 'Imperial Preference' – this was the system of preferential trade tariffs, effectively free-trade agreements allowing goods and services to be traded within the empire at a lower cost than outside of it. Remember this concept of 'Imperial Preference', when considering if Empire ever ended, or simply evolved.

As the new predominant military and economic power, the US laid down the agenda for the international political economy, and pushed forward the so-called 'liberal and free trade' economic policies it desired.[4] Despite Churchill's protestations to maintain 'the fullest possible rights and liberties over the question of Imperial Preference', the Bretton Woods conference established:

- **The International Monetary Fund (IMF)** – ostensibly to manage interest rates between member states.
- **The International Bank for Reconstruction and Development (the World Bank)** – to provide loans to countries devastated by the Second World War.
- **The General Agreement on Trade and Tariffs (GATT – later to become the World Trade Organization)** – to ensure free-trade economic policies were implemented by member states.
- **Fixed Exchange Rates** – all currencies would be valued in US dollars and the dollar value would be set by gold. The US promised to convert dollars into gold on demand. This was commonly referred to as 'the gold standard'. At this time the US held 75 per cent of the world's gold reserves.[5]

By 1971, the Bretton Woods system had contributed to the successful reinvigoration of Western economies devastated by World War Two, but there had not been enough gold made available to account for this growth and the value of US stocks had dropped from $25 billion to $10 billion.[6] President Nixon announced that the US would no longer convert dollars into gold, and interest rates were set to float against each other once more.

The rest of the Bretton Woods infrastructure remains intact, and continues to set the roadmap for domestic and international economic policy to this day.

These institutions would ultimately transform empire from the colonial statist model to an internationalized corporate model – with the structural power of the state used to enforce the corporate empire. In short, they have overseen the transfer of power from the State to private institutions and corporations.

This is the endgame of the neoliberal project – whether the key players know and intend it or not.

The rise of the IMF – keeping the benefits of empire

The International Monetary Fund (IMF) invented Austerity. The IMF rose in prominence amidst decolonization, touted as a means of providing monetary assistance to fund the conversion of post-colonial societies into neoliberal democracies.

In reality, the IMF has used predatory lending (often to tyrannical regimes) in order to retain control of the assets, national resources, cheap labour and corporate monopoly that the colonial powers held before decolonization. The colonial powers replaced the shackles of slavery and state colonialism with the Debt Trap.

To understand the profligate lending practices that resulted in the Debt Trap, we need to shift our attention to the 1970s. In 1973, the Organization of Petroleum Exporting Countries (OPEC) was established. OPEC states deposited their oil wealth in Western banks, and high inflation in the West at the time meant that this stored money was losing value.

To make this money work for them, the banks began a lending spree across what was then called the Third World – mostly funding undemocratic regimes and unworkable projects. As far as the Western banks were concerned, the end results of the loans were irrelevant; the purpose was to cash in on the oil money rather than let it devalue in the vaults.

The decade then witnessed a series of oil shocks, which saw the price of oil rise by more than 500 per cent.[7]

The first oil shock took place in 1973. The Organization of Arab Petroleum Exporting Countries (OAPEC) announced an embargo on oil supply to Western nations after the US backed Israel in the Six Day War. This was OAPEC using its role as chief energy supplier to the world to exert political sway and isolate Israel, which it considered a belligerent state of questionable legality.

The price of crude oil soared from \$3 to \$12 a barrel.[8] The impact on the UK economy was significant. The rise in petrol prices made all transport, including industrial, vastly more expensive – which made almost everything more expensive. Inflation soared to 24%.[9] The global reverberations of this economic chaos persuaded US Secretary of State Henry Kissinger to negotiate Israeli withdrawal from parts of the Sinai in Egypt and promise a negotiated settlement between Israel and Syria. These measures secured the end of the embargo in 1974.

Despite the serious global economic impacts of the oil shock, the Western banks continued their feckless lending binge.

The second oil shock took place in 1979, with the fall of the Shah of Iran. It is perhaps hard to imagine now, but at this time Iran was the US's key ally in the Middle East and had been so for a decade. According to a now-declassified report by the US National Security Agency:

'The US had provided material assistance, political and moral support, and Iran had, under a *carte blanche* policy, purchased some of the most up-to-date US weapons systems. Little was said of the Shah's repressive regime.'[10]

During the fall of the Shah, Iranian oil workers took part in national strikes. The result of the strikes was a dramatic fall in oil production and another wave of economic shocks across the industrialized world. There came a domino effect of economic disaster – the US saw trade and budget deficits, most Western economies went into recession, and so demand for exports from the poorer countries fell. As countries' earnings fell, their debt obligations rose, and almost overnight pretty much the entire African and Latin American continents were on the verge of bankruptcy.[11]

This all presented something of a problem for the banks, and the wealthy economies that were benefiting from their profits – what to do?

The IMF became the lender of last resort – and was used to issue bridging loans to these crumbling economies in order that, rather than default on their debts and allow their economies to recover (impacting the West negatively both economically and geopolitically), they would continue to pay back the original loans.

The IMF created a mechanism called the Structural Adjustment Programme (SAP) which meant that emergency loans (to pay off the existing and now unaffordable loans) were granted to 'developing' nations provided the debtor nation subscribed to a range of conditions.[12]

So what do SAPs do? They:

- enforce the selling off of national industries and resources (mostly to foreign-owned corporations and governments)
- remove all capital controls on money flowing in and out of the country
- dictate the level of public spending
- prioritize debt repayments and corporate welfare over infrastructure investment and human welfare, and
- Demand suppression of wages and restrictions on labour unions.[13]

Through the IMF, the creditor nations found a way to impose neoliberal economic policies on foreign populations and sidestep the democratic process in doing so. It was a win-win for the West: there would be no negative repercussions from their lending binge, and the liberalization of the economies guaranteed by the SAPs would have been unthinkable within any democratic context.

The results of the Structural Adjustment Programmes speak for themselves. They have allowed external corporations to make enormous profits by buying up state-owned industries and exploitation rights to natural resources at a low price, while keeping living standards, wages, civil liberties and employment rights low so as to maintain a cheap domestic labour force.[14] The human cost has been felt most painfully in public health. The stipulations to cut spending on health, sanitation and the development of water systems created a public-health catastrophe in the 'Third World'.

According to the World Health Organization:

'In health, SAPs affect both the supply of health services (by insisting on cuts in health spending) and the demand for health services (by reducing household income, thus leaving people with less money for health). Studies have shown that SAPs policies have slowed down improvements in, or worsened, the health status of people in countries implementing them. The results reported include worse nutritional status of children, increased incidence of infectious diseases, and higher infant and maternal mortality rates.'[15]

While crippling the economies of at least two continents, this process has been extraordinarily profitable for the creditor nations and institutions.

The Western creditor nations have consistently resisted the idea of debt forgiveness, arguing that failing to honour debts would encourage further lending and reckless spending by poor states. What they fail to address is that over-borrowing is also over-lending – both sides of this exchange bear responsibility. Yet nothing is being done to prevent the over-lending of these creditor nations.

This comment from Martin Griffiths summarizes the issue perfectly:

'Between 1982 and 1990, $927 billion was advanced to debtor states, but $1,345 billion were remitted in debt service alone. The debtor states began the 1990s 60 per cent more in debt than they were in 1982. Sub-Saharan Africa's debt more than doubled in this period.

'By 1997 Third World debt totalled over $2.2 trillion. The same year, $250 billion was repaid in interest and loan principal. The debt trap represents a continuing humanitarian disaster for some 700 million of the world's poorest people.'

For all 'developing' countries, total external debt owed in 2011 was $4.9 trillion and over the course of that one year they paid $620 billion servicing these debts.[16] In the same year, the total foreign aid supplied to the 'developing world' through the Development Assistance Committee of the OECD was just $133.5 billion.[17]

This means that, in 2011 alone, for every $1 the creditor nations gave the so-called 'developing world' in foreign aid, the debtor nations gave almost $5 back in debt repayments.

The whole premise of international development is called into question when the nations involved are giving with one hand while taking five times as much with the other. Rather than the mainstream narrative – of advanced industrial nations helping to 'develop' inexplicably backward Third World nations, the mask is off. There is no 'developing' world. Instead, there are a host of countries being deliberately decivilized, in order that corporatized states benefit economically and geopolitically. The Debt Trap has been used to reorientate national economies to the service of unsustainable and unethical debt burden, in order to transfer wealth to the creditor institutions and nations.

The financial crisis of 2007/8

It is worth reflecting on the way in which Africa and Latin America were sucked into the Debt Trap when studying the financial crisis of 2007/8.

The decades preceding the crisis had seen long-term collusion between government and the financial-services industry aimed at avoiding proper regulation of financial services in general, and the derivatives market in particular.[18] There was intense lobbying in the US and the UK to maintain this position, with senior government figures on both sides of the Atlantic stepping in directly to prevent the Commodity Futures Trading Commission (in the US) and the Financial Services Authority in the UK from ever coming close to putting the appropriate safeguards in place around these products.[19] This left banks, brokers and insurance companies free to expand their balance sheets rapidly by leveraging debt to almost infinite ratios.

High-street banks and mortgage providers, credit-card companies and other debt merchants chased the custom of individuals with little or no regard for their ability to pay back the loans. They did this to sell on the debts to investment banks as 'collateral debt obligations'. These products were then, with the support of the cartel's gatekeepers, the credit ratings agencies, declared Triple A for their credit worthiness – the same rating as a government bond.

The banks then took these investment products and sold them to the likes of pension companies, which bought them on the basis that they were now deemed perfectly safe.

The same investment banks then insured themselves against the very product that they had just sold the pension firm going toxic. These insurance policies are called 'credit default swaps' (CDS). There was no limit on who could set up a CDS either. So banks could inject greater risk into the market by betting not only on their own toxic sell-offs, but also on those of other banks.

This is the equivalent of an estate agent selling you a house, knowing he had set a fire under the floorboards, then taking out an insurance policy on the house being burned down – and then every estate agent in the country doing exactly the same thing.

At every point of these exchanges, significant fees were being handed over, generating paper profits and making balance sheets look amazingly positive, with no actual product or service underpinning them.

Finally, in 2007, all those over-leveraged consumers around the world started to find it impossible to repay their loans. Then came the 2007/8 version of the debt trap domino effect. As CDS claims went in, insurers couldn't cope with the financial hit and started to fold; the brokers' balance sheets couldn't take the strain; and the high-street banks, unable to claim from broker, bank or insurer, began to implode too.

However, instead of these corporations simply collapsing, this extraordinary mountain of toxic private debt was converted into public debt by the Bank Bailout.

According to the National Audit Office, The UK National Debt rose by £850 billion as a result of the Bank Bailout.[20] This is almost twice the nation's total annual budget. For this amount, the UK could have funded the entire NHS (£106.7 billion a year) for 8 years, its whole education system for 20 years (£42 billion a year) or provided 200 years of Job Seekers' Allowance (£4.9 billion a year).[21]

Structural Adjustment Programmes are now being rolled out across Europe, disguised as 'Austerity programmes' – to reorientate European economies toward servicing the debt economy. Central banks are lending to stabilize national economies that have been broken by the cost of bailing out other banks. The central banks make these funds contingent upon the national government imposing an Austerity programme.

The financial crisis, which was in fact the consummate failure of the neoliberal project, was instead hijacked to accelerate it.

Austerity is Structural Adjustment with a new name.

As with the creation of the Debt Trap that plagued African and Latin American countries, the main consideration here has been the continued profitability of the biggest banks and corporations – not the socio-economic conditions of ordinary citizens. In fact, the public interest is often antithetical to the private interest.

The following chapters will detail the dismantling and destruction of each pillar of social democracy, and the devastating consequences for people and the living planet. As you will see, almost none of these demolitions began with the financial crisis or with the entrance of the Coalition government in 2010. Rather, the actions of recent years have quickened the speed of travel along the roadmap put in place in Bretton Woods in 1944.

1 The Federal Reserve retains the full transcripts and documentation of the Bretton Woods conference, nin.tl/TNpkKh **2** Schuler and Rosenburg, *The Bretton Woods Transcripts* (Center for Financial Responsibility). **3** Source: Hansard, nin.tl/1tfdxF6 **4** Martin Griffiths, *International Relations: The Key Concepts*, Routledge, Oxford, 2008. **5** Ibid. **6** Ibid. **7** John G Ikenberry, 'The irony of state strength', *International Organization*, 1986. **8** Terry Mcalister, 'What Caused the 1970s oil price shock?', *The Guardian,* nin.tl/1tfLc1g **9** The oft-referred-to three-day week and union battles of the 1970s (which Margaret Thatcher leveraged to usher in the neoliberal project) all stemmed from the oil shock. The union battle for higher wages was about workers seeking to ensure their incomes kept pace with ever-increasing inflation. **10** US National Security Agency, 'The Fall of the Shah of Iran: A Chaotic Approach', nin.tl/TNpvoM **11** Griffiths, op cit. **12** globalissues.org nin.tl/TNpAsF **13** World Health Organization, nin.tl/1tfecGs **14** globalissues.org op cit. **15** World Health Organization, op cit. **16** Jubilee Debt Campaign. **17** OECD, nin.tl/TNpTnl **18** Eric Helleiner & Stefano Pagliari, 'The End of Self-Regulation?', nin.tl/1mAE77R **19** my.firedoglake.com nin.tl/1odVE12 **20** UK Channel 4, nin.tl/1mAFq6W **21** Guardian datablog, nin.tl/1odW7QW

2
The rise of the zombie economy

THE process that brought you the financial crisis is now moving into your public services. The real economy is being fed to the Zombie Economy – a night-of-the-living-dead economy that consumes value and defecates debt. It is important to understand what the Zombie Economy is and how it functions, before we move in to see its insidious effect on the real economy.

Understanding value

If I were to take a stone and fashion it into a tool, I might be able to trade it on at a higher value than the original stone. This is because I have added value to the stone, it is now more useful within my community than before and this is confirmed by its increased market value. In short:

A Good Idea + Skill + Usefulness = Added Value

This is the simple equation that most people have in their mind when they think about capitalism. This equation is also key to the social acceptance of the profit principle and the inequality of wealth. People feel that those who add value should be rewarded.

The problem is, this has ceased to be the way our economy has actually worked for some considerable time (if it ever was) – at least from the establishment of Bretton Woods to this day. The way most wealth is accumulated today is not based on this simple premise of adding value by creating something useful and being rewarded for that contribution.

Let's take water as an example. Water has immense value, but only as much utility as there are people who need to drink it, or use it in other ways. So how do you keep increasing profits on water in an economic system that demands infinite growth?

First, as a water magnate, you can set out to buy it all and gain control over the total water supply and production.

You succeed. Now you've increased your customer base. But, now what? Hmm.

You get people to pay you to have 'shares' in the proceeds from what people pay for their water and these shareholders and others run the company.

You succeed. You retain control over the company, you continue to receive profits, and you don't have to do all the work any more. Now what?

You can have people bet on whether the price of water will rise or fall. You realize you can manipulate the price of water at will by creating scarcity or by a whole host of other methods. This means you can ensure the house always wins.

You succeed. You reap more profit. Now what?

You can place your own bets on the stock market with the notional money you've made from all those bets on water prices.

In all this time, the price of water for those using it creeps continually upward. The consumers have to pay not only for the water, but the profits and losses all the way up this giant chain. They are getting no greater utility from the water. That remains constant. But they are forced through monopoly to pay ever higher prices.

This is how financialization works. It takes something that has utility and, without increasing the utility or adding value, it generates ever greater costs to the users, and profits (in the short term) for the owner.

Once financialization has taken hold, you end up with a 'securitization food chain', which sees value-adding activity subordinated to the servicing of debt created by financialization. In short, you create money by creating debt.

The securitization food chain creates profit rather than added value and looks like this:

Debtor $\longrightarrow$ Creditor $\longrightarrow$ Investment Banks $\longrightarrow$ Investors
>>>Loan Payments>>>

In essence, the Zombie Economy exists to overcome the barriers to capital growth. It creates financial instruments that increase the paper value of an asset (not its utility, which is finite) by financializing it.

However, when this house of cards collapses, which is inevitable, it's the consumers that pick up the bill.

The purpose of financialization, the securitization food chain and the Zombie Economy is for creditors, investment banks and investors to make maximum profits from lending. It is the same cycle that we witnessed with the Third World Debt Trap and the lead-up to the financial crisis. The purpose is to move people away from making money by producing things, towards making money from money. The problem is that the debtors (consumers, taxpayers or nation-states) eventually exist solely to service these loans and production becomes secondary.

This is the food chain that has moved into the fabric of the British state, and is now feeding on our public services. One vehicle, more than any other, has enabled this parasitic relationship: the Private Finance Initiative.

The Private Finance Initiative

The Private Finance Initiative (PFI) was initially designed by Chancellor Norman Lamont during the Conservative government of John Major in 1992, and was rapidly expanded under the New Labour government of Tony Blair and Gordon Brown between 1997 and 2009. It was touted as a form of 'public private partnership' whereby the government uses private finance, rather than raising funds through the gilt market.

Since 1992, the vast majority of our hospitals and schools have been built in this way.

PFI loans carry at least twice the rate of interest of gilt-based borrowing and are repaid over 25-30 years.

An August 2011 report by the Treasury Select Committee condemned the Private Finance Initiative, as 'always... more expensive than government borrowing'. Furthermore, the report continues, 'we have not seen clear areas of savings and benefits in other areas... quality was lower in PFI buildings [and]... PFI is also inherently inflexible, especially for NHS projects'.[1]

The report did identify major 'benefits' of PFI to governments that were unrelated to absolute costs or value for money. The majority of PFI debt does not appear in government debt or deficit figures. The government can therefore use it to bury the true debt burden. Government departments can use PFI to increase their own budgets without dipping into their allotted funds for capital investment.

Another 'benefit' of PFI (from the point of view of the companies involved, that is) is that it allows the private sector to develop the infrastructure to deliver national services while shifting the costs and the risk to the taxpayer. Put another way, the taxpayer is funding the development of a private network of service providers. For it is the loan provider of the PFI scheme (the bank) that retains ownership of the asset (the school or hospital) for at least the term of the loan (25-30 years) or in the case of default.[2]

In fact, it appears the only people who are not benefiting from PFI are the people who are actually paying for it – the public.

The report could not have been clearer: 'These incentives unrelated to value for money need to be removed.' They need to be removed because they create a conspiracy of mutual self-interest between private service providers eager to create new markets in publicly run services, banks seeking to make profits on the financialization of public services, and successive governments seeking to put a gloss on their spending figures. The simple interests of the taxpayer and public-service user –

to get what they pay for – have been quietly abandoned amid this circle jerk of the state, private service providers and the financial services sector.

It is actually in the interests of the private service providers and the banks engaging in PFI for the state to default on its payments. When this happens, they can retain ownership of the asset – the school, the hospital, the road or the bridge. This might draw one to a more sinister interpretation of the 'poor quality procurement methods' used by those responsible for negotiating the PFI contracts.

By September 2011, 22 of the 103 NHS trusts to enter PFI were facing financial difficulty due to the exorbitant PFI repayments. Some hospitals are having to hand over a fifth of their annual budget to pay for their PFI contracts.[3]

In education, meanwhile, England was estimated to have a shortfall of 250,000 school places for its children by 2014,[4] while the taxpayer has picked up a bill of £70 million for PFI schools that have already closed.[5]

Overall, for a capital investment of £54.7 billion (that's how much money the UK government actually borrowed to build stuff), the taxpayer will pay back an astounding £301 billion over 25 years. Given what we have already seen, many of the 771 PFI projects currently running will bust the budgets of these public services long before then, leaving us with the debt but not the service.[6]

The average profit for a bank on an equivalent capital investment project would be between one and two per cent. A recent report by the European Union Services Strategy Unit (EUSSU), showed that the average profit for banks in PFI projects is over 50 per cent.[7]

So why is PFI so profitable for the banks?

First, as we have seen above, the interest rates on the loans are enormous. At double the cost of ordinary government borrowing they are the equivalent of using a credit card to build our hospitals and schools.

Second, the 'special purpose vehicles' or shell companies set up to manage the PFI projects are generally based in offshore tax havens. As such, these taxpayer-funded enterprises are themselves exempt from paying tax.[8]

Needless to say, banks have become heavily engaged in chasing the PFI pound. At least 91 pieces of public infrastructure are now owned in this way. HSBC has a controlling stake in 27 PFI projects, predominantly schools and hospitals.[9] It is now the outright owner of three NHS hospitals in Barnet, Central Middlesex and West Middlesex. Barclays has joined HSBC in aggressively chasing the PFI pound, setting up its own wealth fund on the back of this rigged market.[10]

As a sign of things to come, one might look at Barnet Council's 'easy council' outsourcing project, which sees 70 per cent of the borough's services handed out to the private sector.[11]

Why we should care

Some might well ask – so what? If the services are still free at the point of use, what do we care who provides them? Here are some answers to that question.

- *Financial costs*: The service might be free at the point of use, but it is not free. Our taxes pay for the services. PFI, by the Treasury Committee's own report, is proven not to provide value for money for the taxpayer. These costs are seeing the closures of hospitals and schools. Public services are being bankrupted.
- *Human costs*: There are real human costs when critical public services suffer the impacts of a budget crisis. Poor quality control, underqualified staff, overworked staff, faulty equipment and so on.
- *The economy, stupid*: Historically, a national construction project would have created jobs in a domestic construction industry, profits for domestic building and services firms, would have remained a publicly owned asset and would have provided tax revenues for the Treasury. In this new model of financialization, the taxpayer pays double the normal costs

for the building process, while the profits and in many cases the assets themselves go to an offshore company, which is not eligible to pay taxes in the UK. This means that, rather than funds recycling within the national economy, they are siphoned out.

- *The endgame*: The endgame is to break public services by financializing them to bankruptcy, and at the point of failure to replace them entirely with privately owned, profit-making services.

Bizarrely, despite the costliness and inefficiency of PFI projects having been manufactured for the benefit of private companies, the PFI and financialization scandals are used by those vested interests as a case for *more* privatization. They are turned into proof positive that publicly run services are inherently inefficient, bureaucratic and costly. The solution put forward by proponents of the neoliberal project is to allow the market (those same banks and private service providers who bankrupted the services in the first place) to take over entirely.

But the project continues apace, and is likely to reach more deeply into our public services over the coming years. At the same time as increasing the burden of debt servicing upon local authorities, central government is reducing the funding it provides to local government by £7.6 billion (26 per cent) by March 2015.[12] This scissoring of local government budgets means the choices will be stark and failure inevitable.

A closer look at each of our public services in turn in the next few chapters will reveal the extent to which the Zombie Economy is devouring them.

1 House of Commons Treasury Committee, nin.tl/1nKvlok **2** John laing, nin.tl/1nKyTHo **3** bbc.co.uk/news/health-15010279 **4** Ian Withers, 'Urgent need for 250,000 school places', Building.co.uk, 18 March 2013, nin.tl/1lJbJeO **5** *Daily Telegraph*, 26 Jan 2011, nin.tl/1nKwyvY **6** *The Guardian*, 5 Jul 2012, nin.tl/1lJcGUf **7** European Services Strategy Unit nin.tl/1nKxh0i **8** Bureau of Investigative Journalism, 4 Sep 2012, nin.tl/1lJdrwt **9** Globalise Resistance, 8 Jun 2011, nin.tl/1nKxLDq **10** barclaysinfrastructurefunds.com **11** *The Guardian*, 23 Aug 2012, nin.tl/1nKy5lM **12** National Audit Office, nin.tl/1lJenRI

3
The destruction of the NHS

THE National Health Service (NHS) celebrated its 65th birthday in 2013. While politicians cut celebratory ribbons and theoretical cake, they were also busy cutting the lifelines that make the service viable. Ceaseless scare stories; never-ending costly reorganizations; rampant commercialization and privatization; and the deliberate loading of unsustainable debt onto hospital balance sheets: these acts are killing the NHS.

Life before the NHS

The National Health Service was born on 5 July 1948 – within the living memory of many alive today. The only recognized health system in Britain prior to the NHS was the system of National Health Insurance, established by Lloyd George from 1911.[1] This insurance was paid by working people and their employers at a flat rate rather than graduated to account for differing levels of wealth; the lord and the labourer paid the same fee. It also failed to cover dependants so that wives and children were left unprotected. Instead, the masses were at the mercy of others. An uninsured person could only gain treatment at a public hospital if they had tuberculosis.

There was a patchwork of voluntary hospitals where those who could not afford private medical care might receive treatment if they could gain sponsorship or philanthropy.[2]

If all else failed, some workhouses had their own infirmaries.[3] Or you died.

The public-health impacts of only accessing healthcare if you were able to pay were very real:

- Every year, thousands died from treatable diseases – pneumonia, diphtheria, polio, meningitis.
- Around 1 in 20 children born in the UK died before their first birthday.[4]
- Those who could not afford to 'call the doctor out' instead endangered themselves with bogus home remedies ranging from the ineffective to the downright poisonous.
- Throughout the first half of the century, the 19th-century view that philanthropy alone could deliver the public-health needs of the nation came under severe challenge.

Over a period of 20 years, a series of events and contributions paved the way for the NHS:

- The 1920 Dawson Report put forward the case for a national service under a single authority.[5]
- In 1926, a Royal Commission on National Health Insurance pioneered the idea of a health service funded by the public.[6]
- During World War Two, the UK government took ownership of the medical service for the first time with the Emergency Medical Service – this catalysed the momentum for a nationalized health service.[7]
- In 1941, a government-commissioned Independent Inquiry established that there were vast inequalities in healthcare provision across the country and across class.
- Finally, the 1942 Beveridge Report into social care put forward the National Health Service as one of the three pillars of a workable social-security system.[8]

Despite a popularity rating of 83 per cent, Britain's victorious wartime leader Winston Churchill led the Conservative Party to one of its greatest-ever defeats in the 1945 general election.[9] He lost to a socialist Labour Party, led by Clement Attlee, and the key issue at the election was social reform and the implementation of the Beveridge Report.

While world leaders were meeting in Bretton Woods to ensure their post-War economic survival, the working classes of the UK had been meeting in working men's clubs, churches and community centres. They did not want a return of unrestrained capitalism, they did not want a government in thrall to big business; they wanted to enjoy the benefits of their hard work. While Labour promised to implement the Beveridge Report in full, Churchill referred to Beveridge as 'a windbag and a dreamer'.[10]

Birth of the NHS

Two White Papers later, and the NHS was born under the auspices of socialist Labour Health Secretary Aneurin Bevan on 5 July 1948. For the first time anywhere in the world, healthcare was based on citizenship, not ability to pay. This meant that any person born in the UK was eligible to entirely free healthcare including access to general practitioners (GPs), hospital treatment, ambulance services, opticians, midwifery and prescribed medicines.

There were queues filling whole streets outside GP surgeries, hospitals, opticians and other service providers the day the NHS was born – and for a while after. It was a moment the tide turned in Britain towards a more equal, collaborative society respectful of everyone's contributions.

There are a plethora of achievements in public health and scientific understanding that were all made possible by a publicly funded national health service.

- Vaccinations for polio and tuberculosis have virtually eradicated these once-common killer diseases.
- Average life expectancy has extended by over 10 years in the UK.[11]
- Between 1950 and 1955 infant mortality in the UK dropped from 1 in 20 to 3 in 100. Today, it stands at 5 per 1,000.[12]

The public health goldmine

Despite all this shared success, there is a huge amount of wealth that could have been made on the backs of the sick. To some, this has been a missed opportunity. In the 65 years since the inception of the NHS, therefore, private enterprise has been seeking a way back in.

The NHS today employs 1.7 million people – only the Chinese People's Liberation Army, the Wal-Mart supermarket chain and the Indian Railways directly employ more people in the world today.[13] The NHS treats over three million people each week, in England alone. The NHS budget in its first year was £437 million (£9 billion in today's money) whereas for 2012/13 it stood at just under £109 billion.

The nation's sick are a potential goldmine for the private medical industry. For all our complaints about waiting lists, uncaring nurses, ambivalent doctors and horrible food, Britain loves its National Health Service. In the last 25 years, it has saved more lives per pound spent than any other health service in the world – except that of Ireland.[14]

Given its success, no government has ever been able even to whisper the idea of privatizing healthcare. We sold the gas, the coal, the water, the phone service, the postal service and the railways. But there has never been anywhere near substantial support for selling the NHS and moving to a system of privately run healthcare.

With a population stubbornly attached to their publicly funded institution, what were successive neoliberal governments and private healthcare providers to do? Privatize by stealth.

New Labour, Tories, Lib Dems: all outsourcing it together

The National Health Service is being gutted by endless and costly reorganizations, rampant commercialization and unaffordable Private Finance Initiative (PFI) contracts.

The latest major reorganization of the NHS, under the Health and Social Care Act, will suck another £4 billion out of the health service. This comes on the back of the £780 million blown by New Labour on 70 reorganizations in just four years between 2005 and 2009.[15] Anyone experienced in change management can tell you that this level of change, which does not allow for new systems and processes to bed in or for their benefits to be measured, is simply madness.

Each of these reorganizations has been centred not on the patient, but on vague concepts of 'choice' and 'competition'. These are euphemisms for privatization – they have attempted to force open a closed market to the private sector despite the UK citizenry consistently supporting public-service healthcare.

There is a growing trend across the country for NHS Trusts to become mere managers overseeing almost entirely privatized healthcare. To give just two examples:

- Southampton Primary Care Trust has outsourced a third of its elective procedures to private providers.[16]
- Serco was recently awarded a £140-million contract to deliver all of Suffolk's community health services.[17]

In both cases, these privatizations have led to serious performance issues and large reductions of staff.

A report by corporate finance consultancy Catalyst, published in September 2012, estimated that newly privatized healthcare services will be worth up to £20 billion over the next few years.[18] Private health companies Circle, Virgin Care and Serco won contracts worth £700 million to provide NHS services in 2013 alone. NHS outsourcing to private providers rose by 10 per cent in 2012, and is set to increase to 40 per cent of all services by 2020.[19]

The S75 Regulations of the Coalition government's Health and Social Care Act will deliver the NHS into the hands of these private companies. These new 'Competition Regulations' force the NHS to put all but a tiny minority of services out for competitive tender. The majority of services currently run by the NHS will shortly and swiftly be turned over to profit-making private-healthcare providers. This is what is meant by privatization by stealth.

Self-interest over public interest

The reality is that, wherever we look, all our major institutions meant to protect and serve the long-term public interest are stuffed with individuals who have abandoned this role in favour of their own short-term self-interest. The NHS story is, sadly, no different.

The MPs and Lords drafting and voting for privatization legislation have a personal financial interest in the outcome. Research bloggers Social Investigations produced an excellent piece of investigative journalism in 2013, revealing:

- 206 parliamentarians have recent or present financial private healthcare connections;
- 142 Lords have recent or present financial connections to companies involved in healthcare;
- 124 peers benefit from the financial services sector;
- 1 in 4 Conservative peers have recent or present financial connections to companies involved in healthcare;
- 1 in 6 Labour peers have recent or present financial connections to companies involved in healthcare;
- 1 in 6 crossbench peers have recent or present financial connections to companies involved in healthcare;
- 1 in 10 Liberal Democrat peers have recent or present financial connections to companies involved in healthcare;
- 64 MPs have recent or present financial links to companies involved in private healthcare;
- 79% of these are Conservative.[20]

Placing self-interest over the public interest in matters of health has far-reaching and potentially catastrophic human costs.

The human cost of failure

There have been two recent examples that act as warning signs of the human costs that flow from failing to protect the public interest.

The Mid Staffordshire scandal

The Mid Staffordshire Foundation Trust consists of two hospitals serving 276,000 people.[21]

In efforts to cut back on staff and other costs in order to gain Foundation Trust[22] status, the Trust placed financial imperatives above the lives and dignity of patients.

Stafford Hospital launched the 'Clinical Floors Project' in order to legitimize reducing the numbers of trained nurses operating the wards. In fact, when presenting the proposals to the Hospital Management Board for 'clinical floors', it was estimated that it would produce a saving of £325,000 a year (out of a total £580,000 savings the Board was looking to make). The 'clinical floors' model configured the management of patients by floor, rather than by ward. On Floor 2 at Stafford Hospital, this resulted in just three nurses covering two wards containing a total of 40 patients with gastroenterological and respiratory problems.[23]

The Emergency Assessment Unit is where patients arrive in acute medical crisis and are yet to receive their diagnosis. At such a dynamic and unstable point in their care, a nurse-to-patient ratio of 1:6 was promised – yet at Stafford the ratio dropped to just 1:15.[24]

In order to shed another 21 nursing positions and save a further £594,000, the hospital management board opted to amalgamate surgical wards into 'surgical floors' too, despite warnings from nursing and surgical staff that this would, amongst other risks, exacerbate issues of infection control, privacy and dignity of patients on mixed-sex wards. These calls for care were ignored against the backdrop of financial pressures to make the savings. The board also changed the standard ratio of qualified to untrained nurses from 60:40 to 40:60 across the hospital.

These decisions resulted in patients with complex needs, who previously would have been looked after by a qualified nurse specializing in their condition, now being tended by overstretched, untrained junior staff. In order to save greater funds, the Board then took the decision to reduce its nursing staff by another 52 posts, despite a review finding that the nursing establishment of the hospital was already understaffed by 77 posts.

We will likely never know the true number of deaths resulting from these failures, nor the human harm of such denigrating treatment while people were at their most vulnerable. We do know that between 400 and 1,200 excess deaths occurred at the hospital throughout this period – rates of mortality that were 27-45 per cent higher than the Health Care Commission's standard mortality ratios.[25]

Despite this, Mid Staffordshire gained Foundation Trust status, as incentivized by the New Labour government on 1 February 2008. Monitor, the gatekeeper of Foundation Trust status, claimed:'The assessment process is critical; robust and careful assessment will ensure that financially sustainable, well-governed NHS Foundation Trusts with responsible management are established.'

However, after the Health Care Commission report in 2010 discovered higher than usual death rates among patients at Stafford Hospital, the subsequent investigation uncovered one of the most distressing healthcare scandals in the life of the NHS. Two inquiries have so far been held to establish exactly how such disastrous conditions were permitted to continue for so long. This comes from the report by the full public inquiry later called by then Health Secretary Andrew Lansley:

'Between 2005 and 2008 conditions of appalling care were able to flourish in the main hospital serving the people of Stafford and its surrounding area. During this period this hospital was managed by a Board which succeeded in leading its Trust (the Mid Staffordshire General Hospital NHS Trust) to Foundation Trust (FT) status. The Board was one which had largely replaced its predecessor because of concerns about the then NHS Trust's performance. In preparation for its application for FT status, the Trust had been scrutinized by the local Strategic Health Authority and the Department of Health. Monitor (the independent regulator of NHS Foundation Trusts) had subjected it to assessment. It appeared largely compliant with the then applicable standards regulated by the Healthcare Commission. It had been rated by the NHS Litigation Authority for its risk management. Local scrutiny committees and public involvement groups detected no systemic failings. In the end, the truth was uncovered in part by attention being paid to the true implications of its mortality rates, but mainly because of the persistent complaints made by a very determined group of patients and those close to them. This group wanted to know why they and their loved ones had been failed so badly.'[26]

In short, every single regulatory body and organization of oversight failed. The results were as follows:

- Patients were left in excrement in soiled bed clothes for lengthy periods;
- Assistance was not provided with feeding for patients who could not eat without help;
- Water was left out of reach;
- In spite of persistent requests for help, patients were not assisted in their toileting;
- Wards and toilet facilities were left in a filthy condition;
- Privacy and dignity, even in death, were denied;
- Triage in A&E was undertaken by untrained staff;
- Staff treated patients and those close to them with what appeared to be callous indifference.[27]

The Second Inquiry Report, while adopting the usual scattergun approach to apportioning accountability (everyone and no-one is to blame), stated categorically: 'Management thinking during the period under review was dominated by financial pressures and achieving FT status, to the detriment of quality of care.'

A similar nightmare to Mid Staffordshire may well be unfolding in other Trusts across the country, with several reports of higher-than-expected mortality rates reported on an almost weekly basis.

The healthcare disaster in Mid Staffordshire should stand as a stark warning: prioritizing the financialization of a service over its core purpose (helping people) costs lives. Real people get poor quality care and die as a result.

Hinchingbrooke

The case of Hinchingbooke Hospital demonstrates the futility of following the government ruse of sending in the private sector to 'save the NHS'.

At the end of 2011, Hinchingbrooke Hospital in Cambridgeshire became the second UK hospital given over to be run by a private company. Hinchingbrooke, stricken with £40 million of PFI-related debt, was ruled to be a failing hospital.[28] In February 2012, Circle, a private healthcare provider, was granted a 10-year franchise to operate the hospital. Circle argued that it could pay off the £40-million debt, make a profit, and raise quality and performance at the hospital. When asked how, the only answer coming back from then chief executive Ali Parsa was greater involvement of doctors and nurses in problem solving.[29] But handing over to the private sector has resulted in continued declining standards and escalating debt.

Circle's debt-reduction plan of £311 million over 10 years relies on job cuts, increasing the number of private patients, reducing nurse-to-bed ratios and streamlining Accident and Emergency. This is the exact model that Stafford Hospital adopted, and which led to such disaster. On top of this, Circle are allowed to keep the first £2 million of surpluses each year, and only receive a sliding scale of profits after that. This means Circle are effectively incentivized to target their £2 million, and could make this profit each year of the contract while never paying down the debt.[30]

In the first six months of the contract, 46 nursing posts were removed. With the hospital continuing to lose money, the chief executives of both Circle and the hospital were replaced in the first year.[31] By February 2013, the Public Accounts Committee had described Circle's debt-reduction plans as 'over-ambitious' and Circle themselves had admitted they might be unable to pay down the debt.[32] While there were initial and short-lived improvements in clinical outcomes at Hinchingbrooke in its first year, there was worse news to come once the results of further cutbacks set in. In October 2013, hospital regulator the Care Quality Commission (CQC) found that the Children's Ward at Hinchingbrooke failed to meet national standards of quality and safety.[33] The CQC found staffing levels below the minimum standards of the Trust, leading to lapses in nursing care and documentation. This included patients not having their fluid intake monitored, while doors to a storage room containing medical equipment, including knives, had been left open.

It all sounds achingly familiar.

Inside the NHS, hundreds of thousands of healthcare professionals are trying to save or improve lives, while the financial resources meant to be at their disposal are being consumed by this process of financialization. So why aren't they sounding the alarm?

A conspiracy of silence

In the summer of 2013, a Freedom of Information request revealed that 52 NHS staff have been paid £2 million by their hospitals in gagging orders that ban them from reporting significant failures of private healthcare providers operating NHS contracts against the public interest.[34] The head of NHS England, Sir David Nicholson, had previously testified before the Public Accounts Committee that no such orders had been issued.

Tory MP Steven Barclay, a leading member of the Public Accounts Committee, accused Sir David Nicholson of either failing to ask the appropriate questions of his staff, or being 'complicit in a cover-up' of failure and paid-for silence within the increasingly privatized NHS.[35]

Previously in March 2013, Health Secretary Jeremy Hunt had been forced to ban the use of gagging orders in the NHS after it was revealed that more than £15 million had been spent silencing 600 NHS staff.[36] However, this figure did not include 'judicially mediated' gagging orders – those that had been signed off by a judge or senior lawyer, rather than the Department for Health.[37] At the time of writing, it has been discovered that 52 such orders have been made, some costing the taxpayer as much as £500,000.[38]

This is in stark contrast to Sir David Nicholson's previous testimony to the Public Accounts Committee, also in March 2013, when he stated that he had only come across one instance of such orders, indicating they were extraordinary measures rarely employed.[39]

In June 2013, North East Cambridgeshire MP Steven Barclay told the *Daily Telegraph*: 'It is simply not plausible that the man who was supposed to be running the NHS was seemingly unaware that employees threatening to speak out were being offered golden goodbyes in return for a vow of silence... What patient safety concerns have been covered up [by these gagging orders]? How many lives have been put at risk?'[40]

At the time of writing, we do not yet know what these staff were paid to remain silent about, but given that people were not paid to remain silent about some appalling recent discoveries, we should brace ourselves for the worst.

In 2012, Serco – the private firm delivering out-of-hours GP services in Cornwall – admitted it had grossly understaffed its service, failed to meet performance targets and so falsified more than 250 reports to the NHS. The firm had essentially lied to the NHS about completing procedures, calls and follow-ups, which it had neglected to perform. It was discovered later that the contract with Serco provided no mechanism by which the firm could be fined, let alone removed, so the company remains unpunished, delivering a service that it has demonstrated it is unfit to manage.[41]

Paediatric services (surgery and care of sick children) at the BMI Mount Alvernia hospital in Surrey, which held a contract for referred NHS patients, was found to fail eight out of nine care standards by the Care Quality Commission. The health watchdog discovered what it terms 'life-threatening' failures at the hospital, stating that 'Medical, surgical and some nursing practices at BMI Mount Alvernia Hospital were so poor that people were put at significant risk… One of the most serious concerns was the care of children admitted for surgery.'[42]

The failings included children being operated on without parental consent, a child being given a nerve block on the wrong side of their body before surgery, resuscitation teams failing to respond to emergency calls, and children being operated on by a surgeon without gloves and whose shirtsleeves were stained with the blood of other patients.[43] While NHS referrals to the hospital have ceased, BMI retains its £200-million-a-year contract to provide services to the NHS.[44]

These are just two amid a growing pile of failures for which the NHS is paying, both to rectify medical mistakes made by private firms, or to compensate those who have suffered.

Private firms now have a massive and increasing stake in the NHS. Private firms treat almost one NHS patient in five for certain conditions, carrying out 17 per cent of hip replacements and hernia repairs, 10 per cent of all trauma patients (broken limbs etc) and 6 per cent of all gall-bladder removals in England.[45]

With NHS staff being paid for their silence, how many other failures do we know nothing about?

The entire responsibility for discovering malpractice and underperformance is in the hands of the Care Quality Commission (CQC), which is itself in crisis.

The CQC has little over 2,000 staff; they are responsible for monitoring 174 NHS Trusts, which employ more than 1.4 million staff, and manage 4.6 million NHS hospital admissions leading to surgical care each year.[46]

A staff survey in 2012 found that just 16 per cent of the 1,473 respondents at the CQC felt the regulator was well managed, just 14 per cent had confidence in the decisions made by the executive team and a mere 8 per cent felt change was well managed.[47] An internal review in 2013 also found bullying was 'entrenched' within the watchdog, with 28 per cent of staff reporting a culture of bullying, and 92 per cent stating that they had personally experienced bullying inside the organization.[48]

Yet it is this woefully understaffed, poorly managed unit which is the only system we have for identifying health care failures, while NHS executives pay staff to keep their mouths shut.

The man overseeing this debacle, Sir David Nicholson, was also in charge of the Mid Staffordshire Healthcare Trust at the time that patients were seriously mistreated. Nicholson oversaw the deaths of more than 4,000 people at Stafford Hospital between 2005 and 2009, and police believe that as many as 300 (1 in 14) of these are the result of 'criminal neglect'.[49] Nicholson is not steering the NHS away from the iceberg, he has set a direct course towards it and ordered full speed ahead. And despite this clear breach of patient and public trust, and repeated calls for his resignation – he remained in post. Nicholson was allowed to retire with pension and conditions intact in March 2014.[50]

His replacement, Simon Stevens, is a former health advisor to New Labour and pioneer of much of the financialization and privatization schemes that paved the way for such problems.

Stevens arrives fresh from a position as President of Global Health Division of United Health Group – one of the world's largest private healthcare companies.

The end of the NHS?

As we have seen, the NHS is being outsourced, commercialized and financialized to destruction. When the end comes, the blame will be placed on the public service, not the private parasites. The argument will be made that we can no longer afford our NHS, and the public-health goldmine will be entirely under the ownership of the profiteers.

This same model is being used to undermine not only public health, but also public education.

1 BBC History Extra, nin.tl/1ozq6Hs **2** Voluntary Hospitals Database, nin.tl/ 1lLMqbL **3** workhouses.org.uk **4** BBC news, 1 July 1998, nin.tl/1ozrmdB **5** Interim Report on the Future Provision of Medical and Allied Services (Lord Dawson of Penn), 27 May 1920 **6** The National Archives, nin.tl/1lLNwo6 **7** nhshistory.net/ ems_1939-1945.htm **8** The National Archives, nin.tl/1lLOoZM **9** BBC History, nin.tl/1ozte65 **10** Ibid. **11** BBC news, 27 Jun 2008, nin.tl/1lLP9Ca **12** United Nations World Population Prospects Report 2011 and CIA World Factbook. **13** NHS choices, nin.tl/1ozunKZ **14** Pritchard and Wallace, 'Comparing the USA, UK and 17 Western Countries' Efficiency and Effectiveness in Reducing Mortality', *Journal of the Royal Society of Medicine*, 2011. **15** LSE blogs, nin.tl/1lLQ7yg **16** Out-Law.com nin.tl/1lLQDw7 **17** *New Statesman*, 15 Apr 2013, nin.tl/1ozvTfU **18** Catalyst Corporate Finance, nin.tl/1lLRjS9 **19** Out-Law.com nin.tl/1lLQDw7 **20** Social Investigations, nin.tl/1lLRXPP **21** midstaffs.nhs.uk **22** FoundationTrusts are non-profit corporations. They differ from NHS Trusts in several ways, but the key two are that they are not directed by government and they are free to deliver their services as they wish (as much private borrowing and outsourcing of services as they please). **23** Mid Staffs public inquiry, nin.tl/1ozxVNa p 211. **24** Ibid, p 215. **25** Healthcare Commission investigation, nin.tl/1lLTDZy **26** Mid Staffs public inquiry, nin.tl/1ozxVNa **27** Ibid. **28** HSJ Corporate, 18 Feb 2013, nin.tl/1lLUiAC **29** BBC news, 10 Nov 2011, nin.tl/1ozAsa3 **30** HSJ Corporate, op cit. **31** BBC news Cambs, 25 Oct 2012, nin.tl/1lLVugO **32** HSJ Corporate, op cit. **33** Hunts Post, 25 Oct 2013, nin.tl/1ozBXFi **34** *The Independent*, 12 Jun 2013, nin.tl/1lLWhON **35** Ibid. **36** *The Guardian*, 12 Jun 2013, nin.tl/1ozD73w **37** *The Independent*, op cit. **38** *The Guardian*, op cit. **39** *The Mirror*, 12 Jun 2013, nin.tl/1ozEdfS **40** *The Independent*, op cit. **41** Commissioning .GP nin.tl/1lLYoCk **42** BBC news Surrey, 15 May 2013, nin.tl/1ozFN1i **43** *The Guardian*, 3 May 2013, nin.tl/1lLZoX0 **44** *Daily Mail*, 2 May 2013, nin.tl/1ozGZ4K **45** *Daily Mail*, 14 May 2013, nin.tl/1lM09PT **46** RCS, nin.tl/1ozI4JT **47** *Health Service Journal*, 2 Nov 2012, nin.tl/1nkgyl3 **48** HSJ Corporate, 26 July 2013, nin.tl/1ozJ54A **49** *Daily Mail*, 10 Jun 2013, nin.tl/1lM1LsT **50** NHS England, nin.tl/1rN95ft

4
Privatizing education

SUCCESSIVE UK governments have largely dissolved the model of state-owned schools staffed by public-sector employees. Today, the majority of UK children attend privately owned schools, where the majority of services are delivered by private-sector staff – even though the parents likely believe their child attends a state school.[1] The results have seen costs soar and quality plummet.

Privatization of state schools

Academy schools are publicly funded independent state schools (limited companies) – this means they receive their funding from central government and are accountable directly to central government, rather than to their local authority.[2] Contrary to the 'localism agenda' lauded by both mainstream parties, the trend is towards centralizing control in Westminster. The schools are also able to make changes to staff pay and conditions – in other words, pay them less.

During the 13 years of New Labour government, 203 state schools were turned into academies. By August 2014, after just four years of Coalition government, this figure had jumped more than 14-fold, to 2,941. One might conclude from this that the initial programme was so successful that it called for rapid national roll-out – but one would be wrong.[3]

A recent report by the Public Accounts Committee, the parliamentary select committee responsible for ensuring value for money for the taxpayer, condemned the programme as 'complex and inefficient', leading to more than a billion pounds of overspending.[4] This billion pounds had to be met from the budgets for other non-academy schools. The report does not mince words and reports major issues across the programme, including: poor cost control; a lack of transparency over expenditure; a governance and compliance framework prone to failure (exacerbated by significant staff cuts at the Department for Education); and confusion over roles, responsibilities and accountability.

Yet the programme continues apace. Despite having claimed to protect the education budget, spending figures from 2012 demonstrate that the government is doing quite the opposite. In 2013, the budget for education was cut by 5.7 per cent in real terms.

While infrastructure spending was cut by 81 per cent, and the non-academy schools budget was cut by 4.31 per cent, the budget for academy schools was increased by a whopping 191 per cent.[5]

The state sector is being starved of funds, while the academy sector enjoys a glut of funding, which it spends inefficiently and opaquely.

If this wasn't drain enough, we must add in what was former Education Secretary Michael Gove's pet project: free schools.

Free schools are taxpayer-funded private institutions: mixed-ability schools that receive funding to build and operate from the Department for Education. Free schools are promoted on the basis that teachers, students and charities can set up their own community schools with state financial support but with greater academic and cultural freedom. But free schools can also be set up by private schools, faith groups and even businesses.[6]

In 2011, 24 free schools opened across the country. This more than doubled in 2012, with 55 such schools opening their doors. So far, more than £1.4 billion of capital funding alone has been provided by the taxpayer for businesses to open schools and for private schools to scrap their fees.[7] Like academies, free schools suck funding from the state-school sector.

There is also the issue of oversight. While many echoed the

knee-jerk criticism of local authority oversight of schools, in reality, parents want to know their school is following national standards and they want action taken when schools are found wanting. Free schools are therefore now managed directly by the Department for Education. As academies are also now falling under the Department's direct control, more than 3,000 of the nation's schools are now managed by a handful of civil servants in Westminster. Far from creating more localized governance over schools, Gove actually centralized power – moving it out of local communities and into his own office.

Then there is the matter of performance. Gove received a bloody nose in 2013, when his flagship free school was placed into Special Measures by school inspectors Ofsted. The Discovery Free School in West Sussex was given Ofsted's lowest rating of 'inadequate' and received severe criticism from inspectors. The leadership of the primary school were found by the inspectors to have 'serious shortcomings' and to 'believe the school is far better than it is'.[8]

Further embarrassment was caused by the Al-Madinah Free School in Derby later the same year. Female teachers at the school had a clause in their employment contract compelling them to wear a headscarf while teaching pupils, while lessons were routinely scrapped in favour of prayers and children were banned from reading fairy stories as they were considered un-Islamic. Girls were also made to sit at the back of the classroom.[9]

These are not isolated incidents; a third of free schools assessed by Ofsted have been found to 'require improvement' (failed to reach the grade of 'Good').[10] Therefore these schools perform no better, and in fact marginally worse, than ordinary maintained schools, 74 per cent of which receive a rating of 'Good' or higher.[11]

There is also evidence that free schools are largely a middle-class project and are not being built in areas where the demand is highest. This is contributing to capacity issues in our schools. As a result, 20.3 per cent of primary schools are full or have pupils in excess of school capacity, while 79.6 per cent have one or more unfilled places.[12] These numbers are broadly reflected in secondary education, where there was a shortfall of 250,000 school places by 2014.[13]

In summary, the UK government has removed local control from schools and handed public money to private interests to build and operate them instead. These privately run schools are performing worse than ordinary state schools, and the UK is not building enough schools in the right areas to meet the needs of our children.

Disintegration of the National Curriculum

The National Curriculum has been dismantled as part of efforts to focus on retention of data and facts rather than understanding and creativity. Students also face a decrease in time dedicated to lessons such as drama, art, music and physical education. This was mostly the work of Conservative former Education Secretary Michael Gove, and it is perhaps the development of the history curriculum that provides the best summary of Gove's disintegration of the National Curriculum.

Gove unveiled his new history curriculum in 2013 and with it his plans to reduce the subject to a romp through the stories of Great White Men of the British Isles, and tales of the Empire. This confining of taught history to a tiny island in the Atlantic – albeit our own – will train a generation of schoolchildren for a world that no longer exists, while denying them access to a thrilling world beyond their own doorstep.

Gove made a big song and dance about inviting the likes of Stephen Mastin and Simon Schama to support development of his new, exciting and (buzzword warning) 'rigorous' curriculum. Instead, after a specious and disorganized 'consultation', Mastin reported: 'Between January and the publication of this document – which no-one involved in the consultation had seen – someone has typed it up and I have no idea who that is… There is no world history in there at all except when Britain bumps into these places.'[14]

Professor Schama also rejected the final curriculum, which he claims bears little relation to any advice he provided. Speaking at the Hay Festival, Schama called the curriculum 'insulting and offensive'. He went on to say: 'This is a document written by people who have never sat and taught 12-year-olds in a classroom... None of you should sign up to it until we trap Michael Gove in a classroom and tell him to get on with it.'[15]

Gove demonstrated a stunning inability to work in concert with the teaching profession. When he received criticism for this, he became aggressive and intransigent.

Zero tolerance of criticism

The criticism and warning from those actively involved in the education of our children and young adults has been united, consistent, loud and sustained. It has also been entirely ignored.

A hundred leading education academics wrote a letter to Gove, published in the *Independent* newspaper, condemning the curriculum. They warned that the 'mountain of data will not develop children's ability to think' and that the micromanagement of the curriculum by a few bureaucrats in Gove's office 'betrays a serious distrust of teachers'. The professors and teachers also stated that the net effect would be a 'dumbing down of teaching and learning'.[16]

Gove even garnered the unique accolade of receiving a vote of no confidence from the National Association of Head Teachers. The historically softly spoken union of 28,500 head teachers broke with tradition with this landmark vote to tell the renegade Education Secretary that his reforms were 'not in the best interests of children'.[17]

The UK's three biggest teaching unions passed similar votes at their Easter conferences in 2013.

This was followed up by more than 2,000 teachers putting their names to a petition condemning Gove's 'list of facts' curriculum.[18]

Gove's response to this almost universal rejection of his

policies was to denounce the critics as 'enemies of promise'. In a letter to the *Mail on Sunday* in March 2013, he wrote: 'the new Enemies of Promise are a set of politically motivated individuals who have been actively trying to prevent millions of our poorest children getting the education they need'.[19]

This from the representative of a government that has scrapped the Educational Maintenance Allowance that helped the poorest youngsters stay in education by funding their travel and other costs,[20] binned the Aimhigher Programme that encouraged children from disadvantaged backgrounds to aspire to and prepare for university,[21] and trebled the tuition fees for students attending university. Who is the enemy of promise?

Not only is the government using the 'securitization food chain' to privatize the public education system by stealth, but it is also dismantling the very elements of the system that promote critical thinking, social mobility and aspiration in children. This same approach is being pursued in higher education.

The securitization food chain reaches higher education

In June 2013, the UK government commissioned the Rothschild Bank to develop plans for the sale of student loans taken out since 1998. The Bank recommended retrospectively raising the interest rates paid by graduates, and using tax revenues to guarantee all loans in the case of default to increase the attractiveness of the loan book to private buyers.[22]

If adopted, this would leave 3.6 million graduates facing sharp rises in their student loan repayments, while the taxpayer stands as guarantor in the event students default on the debt, paying up to ensure the private investors never lose a penny. So it is that the securitization food chain reaches higher education – and here is how it works.

Tuition fees

Previously, tuition fees were capped at £3,000 a year. One of the first acts of the Coalition government was to introduce a new ceiling of £9,000 a year (despite a Liberal Democrat pledge to scrap tuition fees altogether) – trebling the potential fees payable by students.[23]

It's hard to believe that, a little over a decade ago, the UK viewed higher education as a social service. We clubbed together to put our young people through university, as an investment in their (and our) future. However, as manufacturing and many non-graduate jobs moved offshore to allow corporations to maximize profits from poor labour conditions abroad (those conditions created by the previous incarnation of IMF-imposed austerity), a pending jobs crisis loomed.

This was the 'changing economy and jobs landscape' Tony Blair was talking about in 1999 which called for his target of 50 per cent of young people attending university.[24] His aim was to put more young people through university and create new graduate jobs for these young people to migrate to. The populace was told that in order to fund this expansion in student numbers, tuition fees were required to spread the burden between taxpayer and individual. A quick look at the facts proves this argument invalid on several grounds.

First, the UK is not a leader of developed nations in terms of the percentage of its population receiving a university education. In fact, between 2000 and 2008 (after tuition fees were introduced), the UK fell from 3rd to 15th in graduate numbers, according to OECD figures.[25]

Second, several nations above the UK in this league table have not introduced tuition fees. In Finland, which tops the league, 80 per cent of young women attend university and there are no tuition fees. Denmark, Sweden and Norway all also outrank the UK and none have introduced tuition fees.[26]

So introducing tuition fees did not increase the UK student population any faster than the rest of the OECD – in fact, it slowed us down. And we can see from examples in other OECD countries that a rising student population does not require the cost of education to be transferred to the student by way of tuition fees. To cap it all, that 50-per-cent target has never been reached. There was no public need for the securitizing of higher education. Nor was there any public benefit to be derived from it – only massive and ultimately unsustainable costs.

Student loans

There have been two distinct phases of student loans in the UK: pre-1998 and 1998-2012.

Pre-1998 student loans were payable over 60 monthly instalments, paid at the rate of inflation, and the debt was cancelled when the graduate reached 50 years old. Between 1998 and 2012, student loans were based on income as a graduate. A graduate would pay 9 per cent of their annual income each year once they earned more than £15,795 a year. Under these loan agreements, interest rates are capped at either the Retail Price Index (RPI) measure of inflation or at banks' base rate plus one per cent, whichever is lower. On student loans taken out since 2012, the interest rate has risen to RPI plus 3 per cent.[27]

The Rothschild Bank's privatization report states that this low interest rate will be unattractive to private investors and so should be scrapped in favour of higher rates, never mind the impact on the graduates who took out these loans under the current interest agreement. According to *The Guardian* newspaper's report on the matter, dated 13 June 2013:

'Removing the cap would, however, burden graduates with years of extra repayments, lasting in some cases until the end of their working lives. At the moment, the cap on student debt taken out before 2012 keeps repayment rates at 1.5 per cent. Lifting it would mean a rate of 3.6 per cent, in line with RPI in March 2012. One indicative calculation suggests that an employee on £25,000 a year, with £25,000 of undergraduate loans taken out before 2012, could work until retirement without ever paying off their debt if the interest-rate cap were removed.'[28]

The Rothschild report goes even further. It also suggests

creating a 'synthetic hedge' whereby the government pledges to underwrite all risk associated with the student debt – meaning that in the case of default, the taxpayer covers the investor's potential losses. Some have argued that since the paper was prepared in 2011, this is old news or unlikely to become policy. Yet early in 2013, the government revealed plans to auction the student loans between 1990 and 1998, for a face value of £900 million (but it is likely to receive just a fraction of this figure). The post-1998 loan book is worth far more than this, at £40 billion.[29]

Furthermore, the government is eager to plug an ever-growing hole in higher-education funding. Back in 1999, on the introduction of fees, the funding agreement for higher education was £4.2 billion a year.[30] If spending had been maintained in line with inflation, this figure would stand at £6.1 billion today. However, funding for higher education in 2012/13 was cut in absolute terms by £1.2 billion, down to just £5.2 billion.[31] This is an enormous real-terms cut in funding, for a much larger pool of students. The government is using securitization to attempt to close the consequent hole in the budget.

The 2012 student-loan agreement saw the minimum earnings threshold required to begin paying back the now bigger student loan raised to £21,000 a year. However, less than a year later, Treasury officials were already demanding this be lowered to just £18,000 a year in order to fill the gap left by spending cuts in higher education.[32]

In the longer term, it is estimated that 39.4 per cent of student loans will never be paid back, as graduates will not earn enough to afford the repayments before reaching the end of the repayment term.[33] Selling the debt to private investors now, and making a future government responsible for the fall-out, would allow the Coalition government (2010-2015) to maintain its failing policies without the consequences becoming clear on its watch. It can sow the seeds for crisis yet will have long moved on by the time the public and a future government reap the whirlwind.

But the cracks are already starting to show:

- Student numbers are lower now than in 2010.
- The UK has a lower percentage of 20 to 29-year-olds enrolled in full- or part-time education than the OECD average – lower than Poland, Estonia, Hungary or Turkey.[34]
- Since 2011, the UK government has actually cut student places by 25,000 and overseen a 40-per-cent drop in applications from mature and part-time students.[35]

Student loans gifted to the private sector have proven fairly catastrophic in the US. Student debt hit one trillion dollars there in 2012, and is now the largest type of consumer debt, second only to home mortgages.[36] The number of seriously delinquent loans – those left unpaid for more than 90 days – has risen to an all-time high of 11 per cent. Worse, a whopping 21 per cent of loans have missed a payment or are not to be paid back at all. This has raised fears that student-loan debt will be the source of the next financial crisis – in effect becoming the new sub-prime lending crisis.[37] Whereas in 2007/8 the taxpayer bailed out banks that had dished out unaffordable mortgages, by 2018 we could be bailing out banks that have dished out unaffordable student loans.

Unaffordable student debt only becomes less affordable when privatized, as interest rates rise. If the state is the ultimate guarantor of these loans then, when the crisis occurs, the taxpayer will pick up a bigger financial burden than if the loans had remained with the state throughout.

What privatization allows, though, is a short-term mega-profit for private investors and a short-term fiscal bounce for the sitting government – neither of which will lose out when the crisis comes.

Keeping the powerful honest

Simon Schama concluded his criticism of the assault on the UK education system with the following stirring sentences: 'History is not about self-congratulation. It's not really about chasing the pedigree of the wonderfulness of us... Nor about chasing the pedigree of the reprehensible awful nature of us. History is meant to keep the powerful awake at night and keep them honest.'[38]

Ultimately, the assault on the education system and those who deliver it serves only to diminish the capacity of future generations to fulfil their task of keeping the powerful awake at night, and keeping them honest.

As the Zombie Economy feasts on the securitization food chain in public services, funding is pulled from servicing the real economy to feed it. This results in reduced spending on infrastructure, the salaries and terms and conditions of public-sector workers, and the generosity of the social-security system.

---

1 *The Guardian*, 5 Apr 2012, nin.tl/1rumghw **2** Parliament website, nin.tl/WJtuFj **3** Gov.uk, Sep 2014, nin.tl/1rs9HkR **4** *The Guardian*, 23 Apr 2013 nin.tl/ZC5l4j **5** *The Guardian* datablog, nin.tl/1odW7QW **6** Gov.uk, nin.tl/ZC7sFu **7** Gov.uk, 30 Sep 2014, nin.tl/1ruqwha; Channel 4 Factcheck, 9 Jun 2011, nin.tl/WJuuta **8** *The Guardian*, 19 Jun 2013, nintl/1sFGRUw **9** National Secular Society, nin. tl/WJuZmV **10** Local Schools Network, nin.tl/1rutdzf **11** Ofsted, 25 Apr 2013, nin.tl/WJv9uD **12** Fullfact.org nin.tl/1rutXV8 **13** Building.co.uk 18 Mar 2013, nin.tl/1lJbJeO **14** *The Observer, 16* Feb 2013, nin.tl/1ruv1bF **15** *The Telegraph*, 30 May 2013, nin.tl/1ruw2jW **16** *The Independent* letters, 20 Mar 2013, nin.tl/1nQpSL6 **17** *The Independent* 18 May 2013, nin.tl/1o5Vdp4 **18** *The Independent* 15 Apr 2013, nin.tl/1nQsg4F **19** *Daily Mail*, 23 Mar 2013, nin.tl/1o5VQyS **20** *The Guardian*, 25 Oct 2010, nin.tl/1nQuf9g **21** *The Guardian*, 20 Aug 2011, nin.tl/1o5WjBg **22** *The Guardian*, 13 Jun 2013, nin.tl/1nQvXqW **23** Channel 4 news, 9 Dec 2010, nin.tl/1o5WY5s **24** BBC news, 8 Mar 1999, nin.tl/1o5XsIM **25** BBC news, 3 Nov 2010, nin.tl/1nQz1Dw **26** Ibid. **27** *The Guardian*, 13 Jun 2013, nin.tl/1nQvXqW **28** Ibid. **29** Ibid. **30** BBC news, 8 Mar 1999, op cit. **31** *The Guardian* datablog, 29 Mar 2012, nin.tl/1o60SLD **32** *The Telegraph,* 13 Jun 2013, nin.tl/1nQl8Ec **33** *The Guardian* Professional blog, 17 Jun 2013, nin.tl/1nQJcrD **34** oecd.org/edu/ highlights.pdf **35** *The Guardian* Professional blog, 10 Jun 2013, nin.tl/1nQKV0f **36** *MoneyWeek*, 27 Apr 2012, nin.tl/1o63sS6 **37** Ibid. **38** *The Telegraph*, 30 May 2013, op cit.

5

The assault on social security

ANY social democracy is underpinned by a generous welfare state that ensures citizens who find themselves unable to work through involuntary unemployment, sickness, disability or age receive enough support to live in dignity. Social security means workers are less likely to be exploited by poverty wages, as people are in nations without a welfare state. Social security promises that those who find themselves unable to work are not abandoned to the lottery of charity or philanthropy. Social security creates a guaranteed minimum standard of living for every citizen, regardless of their circumstances of birth. This is what makes it the core offering and foundation stone of social democracy.

Austerity is not so much chipping away at this foundation, as taking a breaking hammer to it. This chapter will cover some of the key changes to social security during the period of austerity, and how these changes are all about making the victims of neoliberalism pay for the crisis.

Workfare

The government has a whole host of 'work programmes' purportedly in place to encourage the jobless back into paid employment.[1] Workfare refers to all of the programmes that are mandatory, long term and paid less than the minimum wage.

No-one is arguing against relevant, short-term work experience, which is a useful offer for both young and mature jobseekers. But offering an unemployed 21-year-old history graduate two weeks' work experience with the British Museum at their request is quite a different proposition from forcing the same 21-year-old into eight weeks stacking shelves at Tesco under threat of sanction.

The government's Work Experience Programme, Sector Based Work Academies, Community Action Programme, Mandatory Work Activity scheme and Work Programme all fall into this latter category.

The Workfare programme was born under New Labour. In that government's New Deal, long-term unemployed people underwent a compulsory 'intensified job search'.[2] If the intensified job search period (lasting up to four months) proved unsuccessful, participants entered the second stage of the programme and were offered one of four options: full-time education or training for 12 months, a job with the voluntary sector for 6 months, work for the environmental task force for 6 months, or subsidized employment for 6 months with provision of employer-managed on-the-job training. This last option was sometimes made available to people before the end of the 'Gateway' period.

On the first three options, individuals continued to receive the equivalent of Jobseeker's Allowance (unemployment benefit). In addition, for working in the voluntary sector or on the environmental task force, they received an extra £400 spread over the six months. The value of the employer subsidy was £60 per week and employers received an additional £750 to cover the costs of the training they were mandated to provide.

In 2011, the Conservative and Liberal Democrat coalition government announced a plan to increase uptake of Workfare by 100,000.[3] They also made changes to the programme as follows:

- A jobseeker who leaves a placement after one week loses their welfare payments for six weeks. If they do this a second time, they lose them for 13 weeks. The third time, three years.

- Placements can be mandated for up to 30 hours a week for as long as 6 months.
- The scheme has been opened up so that corporations in the private sector can exploit this taxpayer-funded, forced labour.

All this means that someone who finds themselves unemployed today must work up to 30 hours a week, for up to six months at a time, stacking shelves for Tesco or Poundland simply to receive as little as the £53 per week to which they are already entitled as part of Britain's social contract.[4] In addition, Tesco isn't paying the £53; the public are, through their taxes.

The Coalition promises an interview at the end of the completed Workfare term – yet it is not required that the Workfare provider should actually have a vacancy. This is often, therefore, an interview for a job that doesn't exist. Government representatives wave this issue away, and claim interview experience is a valuable asset. It is indeed, which is why it was previously provided within the Job Centre as a service – not traded for months of free labour to the private sector.

There are a number of practical and principled objections to Workfare.

First, as a society, **we have agreed that forced labour is against the law**. Article 4 of the European Convention of Human Rights clearly states: 'No-one shall be required to perform forced or compulsory labour'. If the government threatens to withdraw a person's sole lifeline unless they supply their labour, then it can clearly be argued that this labour has been obtained forcibly. The labour is also clearly compulsory.

Second, **allowing public funding of private labour is reverse socialism**. It is completely unconscionable to many, that while the government is taking a chainsaw to the welfare state on the stated grounds of Austerity, it chooses to use taxpayers' money to fund forced labour for private corporations. Aside from the principle of this being abhorrent in and of itself, there are a series of undesirable outcomes. It means corporations get to choose between salaried and free staff, creating competition with the 'real' jobs market and acting as a further means of suppressing wages in the real economy. It also means that tax-avoiding companies such as Topshop owner Arcadia get free staff paid for by taxes that they themselves refuse to pay.[5]

Third, it entirely **subverts the minimum wage**. We agreed as a society that we needed a minimum wage in order to provide a balance between a corporation's logical ambition to reduce its labour costs and a worker's need to gain a fair, living wage. Before and since the implementation of the minimum wage, corporations have battled against this legislation, arguing that they need to be free from this 'red tape' in order to compete and grow their business. The Workfare policy allows corporations to avoid paying not only the minimum wage but any wages at all.

The Bedroom Tax and the housing crisis

The Bedroom Tax stipulates that anyone claiming housing benefit faces cuts in their payments relative to the 'under-occupancy' of their home. Housing Benefit claimants saw their funding cut by 14 per cent if they were deemed as having a 'spare room', 25 per cent for two and so on.[6]

The Coalition government argued that this was not a tax, but the withdrawal of an unfair 'spare room subsidy' enjoyed by benefit scroungers who were wasting taxpayers' money and living in unnecessarily large homes while other poor families endured overcrowded housing.

The Secretary of State for the Department of Work and Pensions (DWP), Iain Duncan Smith, declared the cost of housing benefit unsustainable and argued that the Bedroom Tax was the answer to this problem.[7]

The three pillars of the DWP's argument in favour of the Bedroom Tax are:

- Efficiency – proper allocation of housing to need
- Cost – a reduction in the housing benefit bill to the taxpayer
- Fairness – people not receiving housing benefit have to make

choices about the size of their home based on affordability and therefore so should recipients.

All of which sounds perfectly reasonable, until one looks at the actual cause of the inefficiency, cost and unfairness associated with housing. When those realities are exposed, what we can see is that the Coalition government has taken real grievances about real issues and misdirected reasonable discontent toward the victims rather than the perpetrators.

Social housing: exploding the myths

On the case for efficiency, first let us look at capacity. The UK developed its social housing policy as part of the post-War move to social democracy in the 1940s. Prior to this, the masses were subject to exorbitant rents paid to private landlords that consumed the bulk of their wages, while often living in unsanitary, defunct housing. This experience convinced people that shared, public ownership of housing was essential to ensure decent, affordable homes for all.

The post-War Labour government of Clement Attlee built more than a million homes between 1945 and 1951, with 80 per cent of them being council homes with subsidized rents.[8] This created an abundance of good homes, with rents kept at around a quarter of private-sector rates.

But by the 1979 election, the promise of home ownership was more enticing to the beneficiaries of those council houses than protecting themselves and their families from the ravages of the private sector. Enter Conservative prime minister Margaret Thatcher with the 'right to buy' scheme – the plan to turn the working class into a new propertied class by allowing the purchase (at discount) of council houses. This policy was a manifest failure.

Thatcher supporters act as if the 'right to buy' scheme transformed the class system in the UK and created some sort of egalitarian revolution in home ownership. In reality, home ownership is just nine per cent higher in the UK today than it was in 1979.[9] More than a third of former council houses now sit in the property portfolios of wealthy landlords. In fact, the son of Thatcher's Housing Minister at the time the 'right to buy' scheme was launched became the proud owner of no less than 40 ex-council houses.[10]

The Thatcher, Major, Blair and Brown governments of Conservative and New Labour continued the sale of council housing, while not allowing local authorities to invest the funds from sales into building new homes. In the year 2009/10, just 115,000 new council houses were built, the lowest number in peacetime history.[11] Housebuilding continued to drop and now stands at the lowest level in the last hundred years.[12]

The limited remaining council housing is now rationed out to the poorest of the poor,[13] rather than offered as a service that most can rely on to keep the cost of living within sensible bounds. This has changed the ethos of social housing from a human right, and a part of the package of being a UK citizen, to a last resort.

There were five million people on waiting lists for social housing in the UK in 2013,[14] while the UK continues to build 100,000 homes a year less than it needs to in order to meet requirements.[15] With council-housing waiting lists and mortgages ever further out of reach, everyone else is a hostage to the private rental market.

In summary, decades of defunct housing policy have left the UK with a housing shortage crisis. This is the cause of the 'inefficiency' in the system – a shortage of available housing, and of the appropriate mix of housing, to meet need due to the abandonment of any recognizable public-housing programme.

Second, let's examine the cost of housing benefit.

The post-War housebuilding programme of the Attlee government and subsequent commitments to social-housing policy meant that by 1975, 80 per cent of government spending on housing went on capital investment on the supply side (building and maintaining affordable homes).

By 2000, 85 per cent of government spending on housing went on the demand side, on housing benefit, as the housing shortage allowed private landlords to drive up rents. Today, 40-50 per cent of the average £23-billion housing-benefit bill goes to private landlords.[16]

In October 2012, the National Housing Federation issued a report called *Home Truths 2012: the housing market in England*. The report demonstrated that the housing-benefit bill had doubled in just three years since 2009, as a direct result of the astronomical increase in housing costs.

The findings speak to the dangers of successive governments abandoning social housing to the whims of 'market forces':

- An 86-per-cent rise in housing benefit claims by working families, with 10,000 new claims coming in per month.
- Rents across the UK have risen by an average of 37 per cent in the three years to 2012.
- Between 2001 and 2011, house prices increased by 94 per cent, while wages increased by only 29 per cent.[17]

The rise in housing benefit is coming from escalating private rents outpacing the rise in wages, not from the 'burden' of the jobless. House prices are now 300 per cent higher (in real terms) than in 1959.[18] If the price of a dozen eggs had risen as quickly, they would now cost £19.[19] It is unaffordable and unsustainable, and withdrawing housing benefit from all those who have become dependent upon it does nothing to address the problem.

Once we have examined the issues around efficiency and cost, the question of fairness, as presented by the Coalition government, rings hollow.

Instead of expanding the social housebuilding programme, instead of taking on this cartel of private landlords who are artificially inflating rental prices for tenants who have no option but to pay up, the government is walking away from the problem and blaming the victims. Its proposed 'fair' solution, the Bedroom Tax, is causing utter devastation.

The real impacts of the Bedroom Tax

Inside Housing, a magazine dealing with social-housing issues, reports that the Bedroom Tax will impact 660,000 social-housing tenants, and two-thirds of the households affected will contain a disabled person.[20]

Those impacted lose between £520 and £1,300 a year in financial assistance.[21] For those unfamiliar with being dirt poor, this means choosing between eating three meals a day and having the heating on for an hour in the evening in the winter.

As horrendous as these numbers are, they are just numbers. So here are some true stories that illustrate the real impacts of the Bedroom Tax:

Becky Bell died of cancer at seven years old. Her local council sent her family a £672 bill for her newly empty bedroom.[22]

Vicky Evans, 49, lost both her parents and her brother by her early twenties. Severe anxiety, arthritis and sleep apnoea leave her unable to work. She lives on £101 a week Disability Living Allowance. She has lived in her street for 27 years, everyone knows her and she knows everyone. She feels safe there. She will lose two-thirds of her housing benefit, leaving her unable to afford her house, as it is classed as having two spare rooms. She has been told that if she falls into more than £50 arrears she will be taken to court and lose her home. One might argue that Vicky should simply move to a one-bedroom house nearby. However, there is not a suitable one-bedroom residence within 10 miles of her current home. 'If I have to leave my home and be put away from the places and people I know then I don't know how I'll cope,' she says.[23]

Fred Williams, 59, suffers from cerebral palsy. His two-bedroom home has been heavily adapted to meet his needs. Over 20 years, a stair lift, ramps at the front and rear entrances, an extended and modified kitchen and an accessible shower have all been added to the home. He once shared it with his wife and stepson but after the break-up of the family in 1991 he now lives alone. He is now deemed as 'under-occupying' his home and faces the withdrawal of his housing benefit. Fred has been unable to work since 2006, and he is unable to find a home suited to his needs. He is faced with impending poverty. 'The whole issue surrounding the Bedroom Tax is a con,' he says. '[This] government... is hell bent on making disabled people's lives hell.'[24]

Jayson Lowery, 50, has been the full-time carer for his wife Charlotte since a spinal condition left her mostly confined to her bed. In their two-bedroom flat in Southport, there's a single bed in one room and a specialist NHS-type bed in the other. Charlotte's wheelchair sits there too, cramped in with other medical equipment. Her condition means she can't share a normal bed with her husband and their flat, partly adapted for Charlotte's needs, is too small to put both beds in one room. From April, the couple will lose £12 a week because of this. Despite the fact that Charlotte sleeps in it every night, her room will be classified as 'spare'. Jayson has looked around for something suitable but there simply are no one-bedroom apartments available which would fit both beds and the equipment in one room.[25]

Linda Taylor, 43, and her husband share their three-bedroom home with their severely disabled son Adam. They have become Adam's full-time carers as he has heart, kidney and spinal problems that leave him without mobility. He is incontinent and must be bottle-fed puréed food. The box room is crammed with adult-size nappies, a pressure mattress, Adam's physio equipment and a small bed which a paid carer sometimes sleeps on when overnight care is required. However, this box room is now classed as a 'spare' room and they will lose 14 per cent of their council benefit. 'I feel so frustrated,' she says. 'The only solution I can see is to go and find a job, which I would be willing to do if the council were willing to provide the full care needed for my son... When you can only get 11 hours' care a week we've got no chance of changing life for the better. We're left in a no-win situation.'[26]

Jimmy Daly, 50, has a nine-year-old son with severe

learning difficulties and spastic quadriplegia. He lives between his mum's house and Jimmy's two-bedroom maisonette. Jimmy will have his housing benefit cut because his son does not live permanently in the home. He currently lives on just £71-a-week jobseeker's allowance, and will lose £10 a week in housing benefit. Jimmy and other parents sharing the custody of a severely disabled child are facing the real possibility of being unable to share a home with their child as a result of the Bedroom Tax. 'If this goes ahead I'll have to move into a one-bedroom flat,' he says. 'How do you sleep in the same bedroom as a disabled boy?'[27]

The government's response to these stories has been to tell people to take in a lodger or work extra hours to cover the shortfall in their housing benefit. They are being asked to do the impossible, while their concerns and fears are brushed aside with irrelevant platitudes.

The government promised that its £25-million hardship fund would support all those impacted by the changes.[28] However, according to the government's own impact assessments, 420,000 of the 660,000 people affected by the changes are disabled, and they will lose an average of £14 a week.[29] A moment of arithmetic establishes that this amounts to just under £306 million a year. This means the state has taken £306 million away, and offered just £25 million (not even a tenth of the loss) to compensate the impact. Worse, it is not only disabled people who will require access to this hardship fund but all other impacted groups too, such as foster carers and the working poor.

David Cameron has claimed that parents of severely disabled children would be exempt from the Bedroom Tax. This is not true. The government had been due to change the rules to make this so since May 2012, but the regulations remained unchanged, meaning there was no automatic exemption.

In April 2013, a group of 10 disabled people took the government to court in efforts to highlight the discriminatory nature of the charge. The judge ruled that the Bedroom Tax was indeed discriminatory, but decided that the discrimination was reasonable and therefore lawful. He did, however, find the discrimination against disabled children unlawful and stated that new regulations must be prepared 'very speedily' to ensure that there is 'no deduction of housing benefit where an extra bedroom is required for children who are unable to share because of their disabilities.'[30]

David Cameron claimed that people requiring 24-hour care would be exempt from the Bedroom Tax. This is also not true. While the DWP has made an exemption for people who have a paid live-in or overnight carer, this does not apply if the carer is their partner or spouse. If such a couple share a home with more than one bedroom, they have been charged for under-occupancy since April 2013.[31]

Lisa Evans is the full-time carer for her 25-year-old daughter Vicky, who was left with severe brain damage after an operation as a baby. In 2002, a government grant paid for a two-room extension at their home in Kelfield, between York and Selby, to provide en-suite facilities and specialist equipment for Vicky and a room for a carer.

But the Bedroom Tax saw the mother and daughter's housing costs quadruple, as the government now deemed these alterations as spare rooms and applied the levy.

The Department of Work and Pensions has informed them that they could be moved to a smaller property, but they have no idea where, when or if the new property will have sufficient space and facilities for Vicky's care.

Lisa told the *York Press*: 'If we were to be moved, where would we go? We have no idea where it would be and whether we would have any equipment or transport for Vicky. We would be going to nothing and I feel I wouldn't be able to support my daughter any more.'[32]

Despite the government's claims of safety nets and hardship funds, the tax hit on 1 April 2013 and it hit hard. It also landed at the same time as a raft of other cuts to social security which strike at the exact same groups.

The war on Incapacity Benefit

Government representatives have implicitly and explicitly accused vast swathes of those claiming Incapacity Benefit of faking their illness or disability.[33] Hate crime against disabled people shot up by 25 per cent in 2012, thanks in part to the constant media scaremongering about 'scroungers' faking disability so as to give themselves an easy life.[34]

Atos, the firm contracted by the UK government to perform 'work capability assessments' on all those claiming Incapacity Benefit – before it abandoned the contract in acrimony in 2014 – is never far from controversy.

Atos didn't just enter with the Coalition. It has been the sole private provider of medical assessments for the DWP since 1998. While Atos is the bulldog, it is the ministers of the DWP who hold the leash – and this government has given it a firm order to attack.

The government has required every single person claiming social security payments for sickness or disability to undergo a test with Atos to determine whether they are capable of working. The clear implication is that people should really be working. In fact, ministers have not merely implied this, but have propagandized about it to the point where many people believe it was benefit fraud, and not the Bank Bailout, which caused our sky-high debt.

The government's own statistics show that, between 2010 and 2011, 10,600 sick and disabled people died while going through the Atos assessment process.[35] This is 204 people a week, or 29 people a day. Some 2,200 of these people died before finding out if they were still entitled to their social security, and an astonishing 1,300 had been declared 'fit to work' by being placed in the Work Related Activity Group. These people spent their final weeks alive being harassed by the Job Centre, answering pointless questions, and fretting over late-payment notices and threats of eviction as their social safety net was ripped away.

As this horrific figure of more than one person every hour is almost too large to conceive of, here are some more individual stories.

Linda Wootton, 49, was on 10 medications a day after a double lung-and-heart transplant. She was weak and suffered regular bouts of blackouts. She was put through the Atos 'work capability assessment' and, as she lay in a hospital bed dying, she received confirmation she was 'fit to work'. She died just nine days later. Her husband Peter said: 'I sat there and listened to my wife drown in her own bodily fluids. It took half an hour for her to die; a woman who is apparently fit for work.'[36]

Brian McArdle, 57, had been left paralysed down one side, blind in one eye, unable to speak properly and barely able to eat and dress himself after a stroke on Boxing Day 2011. Despite this, he was deemed 'fit to work' by Atos. He died of a heart attack the day after his benefit payments were stopped. His 13-year-old son Kieran told the *Daily Record*: 'Even though my dad had another stroke just days before his assessment, he was determined to go… He tried his best to walk and talk because he was a very proud man, but even an idiot could have seen my dad wasn't fit for work.[37]

Colin Traynor, 29, suffered from epilepsy. He was deemed 'fit for work' by Atos and forced to enter a lengthy, bureaucratic process to appeal the decision – during which his benefits would be frozen. He did not live to see the result of his appeal. Five weeks after his death, his family received the news that his appeal had been successful. Too late for Colin. His father Ray said: 'I firmly believe – 100 per cent believe – that the system this government introduced has killed my son.'[38]

At the rate at which people are dying, these three people represent the death toll in just the last three hours. This is not just some occasional poor decision; this is a Linda, a Brian, or a Colin, every hour, all day, every day, dying because this system is designed to throw people out of the social-security system – whether they need it or not.

In June 2013, one claimant invited Wirral councillor Joe Walsh and welfare expert Terry Craven to attend his 'work capability assessment'. The Atos assessors refused to conduct the assessment with either of them present, even though claimants are allowed to bring a person into the room. Atos workers then called the police, claiming the two were 'threatening and upsetting people'. Ironic, given the trail of human suffering Atos are meting out up and down the country.

Mr Craven told the *Liverpool Echo*: 'We were just advising people before they went into their medicals of what they should be aware of. A guy asked if we could go in with him and they said "no". I asked on what grounds and they said his benefits might be affected. And when we asked for them to put in writing that his benefits would not be affected by what had happened, they refused.'[39]

Furthermore, the Atos work capability assessments have been roundly condemned as a computer-based exercise unfit to capture the complexity of physical and mental-health issues. Over 30 people have committed suicide, citing stress inflicted by the assessment process, or the impact of cuts as the cause.[40]

Seriously ill and disabled people up and down the country are being harassed, literally to their deaths, by this horrendous excuse for an 'assessment'. However, it is not an assessment if the outcome is predetermined by a quota. The government continues to claim that it hasn't set Atos any target for kicking claimants off benefits – yet multiple investigations have revealed that the company is applying a quota system internally, with assessors rewarded for declaring more people 'fit to work', and penalized for not.[41] The firm would have no reason to behave in this way without a clear steer from the State.

Worst of all, despite claims that this cruel process is an economic necessity, further study reveals that the taxpayer is not getting value for money from this relationship.

A January 2013 report by the Public Accounts Committee, which is responsible for assessing value for money for the taxpayer, found that the taxpayer was not getting a good deal from Atos – and that the responsibility for this lay solely at the door of the DWP.[42]

In 2011/12, the DWP paid Atos £112.4 million to put 738,000 people through 'work capability assessments'. Despite the headlines about how many people were found fit to work by these assessments, the PAC found that 38 per cent of these decisions were overturned on appeal, resulting in court costs of over £50 million.

The Committee also found evidence suggesting that this would worsen over 2012/13, with Citizens Advice predicting a massive rise compared with the preceding year. They were right: appeals rose 70 per cent that year, with benefit appeals constituting 58 per cent of all tribunal cases.[43] After all this, 76 per cent of those who appealed won their cases and were found eligible to receive benefits.[44]

Despite this lamentable performance, the Committee found that the DWP had made no attempt to find a competitor for the contract, meaning Atos had been allowed to continue providing the service for 14 years, without a single challenge from another supplier. The final insult was that the DWP had not even attempted to assess the value for money provided by Atos and had not performed a cost/benefit analysis of the contract. This means neither the government nor the taxpayer knows if this insidious process is saving any money.

Atos receives £206 million a year to conduct these assessments, while its boss earns a cool £2.3 million.[45] The boss's wage alone could fund maximum benefit for 334 people too ill to work.

It is clear that the government is not seeking to increase value for money for the taxpayer. If it were, it would be monitoring this aspect of things. Its priority is rather to transfer public spending from the real economy, where things are made and people are supported, to the Zombie Economy, where profits are made and people are abandoned.

Taking from those with least

One could hardly have imagined in 2010 the sheer scale of horror that would be heaped upon disabled people, their loved ones and carers by the Coalition government. It was hoped that Prime Minister David Cameron – himself touched by the life and death of a severely disabled son – would hold a greater level of understanding of the issues involved. Instead, his government delivered a sucker punch to the community at large.

In 2012, Paralympian and disabled people's advocate Tanni Grey Thompson held an inquiry to examine the impacts of the multiple cuts to social security, the findings of which were produced in a report by The Children's Society and Disability Rights UK. The results were conclusive and devastating, revealing that almost half a million people with disabilities faced losing vital financial and other support as a result of the coming changes.[46] The report identified the three groups most impacted by the changes as:

- disabled people in work
- disabled children and their families, and
- severely disabled people and their carers.

Here are further changes and cuts to social security and the impacts they will have on these groups.

Universal Credit

The brainchild of Iain Duncan Smith, Universal Credit aims to replace a range of social-security payments with one single benefit. However, many existing provisions have been removed or reduced in the new payment.

The new payment makes changes to the Employee Support Allowance and disability elements of Working Tax Credit, removing the financial support that previously allowed some disabled people to work. The payments were designed to reimburse them for the additional costs that arise from being a disabled person navigating a world made for able-bodied people. There could, for example, be additional travel costs for disabled people where public transport is unsuitable. The withdrawal of this support means up to 116,000 disabled people who work losing around £40 a week.[47] In reality, it will make it impossible for some disabled people currently working to continue in their jobs.

The Personal Independence Payment

The Disability Living Allowance (DLA) was replaced by the Personal Independence Payment. Previously, families with a disabled child who received some level of DLA, might have been entitled to support through the disability element of child tax credit, worth £57 a week. Under Universal Credit, this support is to be provided through 'disability additions' within household benefit entitlements, but the proposal is to cut this support in half to just £28 a week. This change will affect all families with a disabled child unless the child is receiving the high-rate care component of DLA or is registered blind. Around 100,000 disabled children stand to lose up to £28 a week.[48]

The new payment also removes the Severe Disability Premium, which provided additional financial support for care required for those with more severe disabilities. As a result, 230,000 severely disabled people who live alone, or with only a young carer – usually lone parents with school-age children – will lose between £28 and £58 every week.[49]

The government's bastardization of the social model of disability is breathtaking – it uses the language of inclusion and empowerment while kicking the ladder out from under an entire community. The result of all these changes is a rising number of people left destitute.

Criminalizing homelessness

The endgame for those who cannot find work, and cannot find shelter, is that they join the ranks of the homeless. There are two types of recognized homelessness in the UK:

- *Statutory homelessness*. These are people deemed eligible for support in finding temporary accommodation funded by their local authority if they find themselves unable to keep a roof over their head. To qualify, a person needs to be eligible for public funds, have a local connection, prove they are unintentionally homeless and demonstrate they are a 'priority need'. Despite the gauntlet one has to run to join this list, the number still rose by 21 per cent in England and 17 per cent in Wales in 2012.[50]

- *Rough sleeping*. This group is formed of all those excluded from the list above, and is very hard to quantify. These numbers have risen even faster, by 31 per cent in England. Homeless charity Crisis claims, however, that numbers could be even higher. Outreach workers in London performed a count which found a 62-per-cent rise in rough sleepers in the capital in just two years.

The government has launched no significant programmes to take action on this issue. Instead, it has chosen to criminalize homelessness through new anti-squatting legislation. The following is the tragic story of just one of the 6,437 people that slept rough on the streets of England during 2012/13.[51]

Daniel Gauntlett, who was 35, froze to death in February 2013 on the porch of an empty bungalow in Aylesford, Kent. He was on the porch because if he had entered the bungalow he would have been in breach of new 'anti-squatting' laws.[52]

In 2012/13, the UK Parliament passed legislation which made it possible for the police immediately to evict anyone found squatting. Since then, there have been 33 arrests, leading to 10 convictions and 3 prison sentences. None of these court cases involved squatters displacing existing tenants; all of the properties involved were completely empty.[53]

Daniel Gauntlett had been one of those arrested, for sleeping in the disused bungalow on a previous occasion. This bungalow was empty, and was due to be bulldozed. On the night in question, Daniel chose to obey the law and settle on the porch for the night, while temperatures dropped to two degrees below zero. This decision to comply with the law cost him his life.

His frigid body was found by a passer-by the following day and an inquest later confirmed he had died of hypothermia.

Daniel was the second homeless man found dead in the town that weekend.[54]

People finding themselves without shelter should be supported by social workers and housing officers, not bullied by bailiffs and police officers. We have permitted our parliament and our police force to criminalize homelessness. This led directly to a young and destitute man freezing to death in the street, while a property lay empty behind him. Sadly, it is not only our homeless people who have been abandoned in the name of Austerity.

The abandoned elderly

Figures released in July 2013 revealed a sharp rise in deaths (five per cent) across Britain over the previous year, predominantly of women over 85 in the poorest areas. Sheffield University's Danny Dorling, who studied the numbers, suggests that the data may portend the first fall in British life expectancy since the creating of the modern welfare state after the Second World War.[55] The Cameron government is effectively addressing the problem of our ageing population by withdrawing the life support of properly funded, qualified and committed care services for old people.

This rise in deaths was exactly what researchers predicted in 2008, after extensive research revealed that the health inequality gap (the difference in life expectancy between rich and poor) in Britain was already bigger than it was during the Great Depression of the 1930s. Their review of deaths between 1921 and 2007 revealed that poor people were dying more often and younger than richer people, and at an ever-accelerating rate. Although life expectancy was rising overall, persistent socio-economic inequalities meant that the life expectancies of the poorest failed to keep pace with the average. Writing in the *British Medical Journal* at the time, the University of Bristol and Sheffield researchers stated:

'By 2007, for every 100 people under 65 dying in the best-off areas, 199 were dying in the poorest. This is the highest relative inequality recorded since at least 1921.' They added: 'The economic crash of 2008 might precede even greater inequalities in mortality between areas in Britain.'[56]

It should therefore come as no surprise that, if poor people were dying at twice the rate of rich people six years ago, this final stage of the neoliberal apocalypse of public services should have exacerbated the situation.

While this affects everyone, it affects the elderly the most. By 2009, the UK's elderly were already the fourth poorest in the EU, behind Romania, with a third of all people over 65 living in poverty.[57] Things have only got worse.

The elderly have now joined the ranks of the sick, the disabled, the young and the unemployed as a 'problem' demographic for our government. Essentially, anyone who isn't in full-time work and earning a taxable income is considered a burden – a drain on the system in these times of Austerity.

This entire line of argument is simply absurd. Our economy needs to fit the demographics it exists to serve, not the other way round. If a person's shoes are too tight, they need bigger shoes. Using this government's logic, the person would be asked to hack off their toes.

An ageing population is not inherently problematic. It only occurs as a problem because of the conflict of priorities (profit versus people) that neoliberalism creates.

The privatization of our core services – energy, transport, utilities, social care, residential homes and nursing homes – has meant that the cost of living for the elderly has risen exponentially. It costs a lot to be old now because we thought it was a good idea to allow people to profit from our most basic requirements – warmth, food and water, shelter and care.

In the UK today, over 90 per cent of all care-home provision – up from 61 per cent in 1990 – for elderly people is in the private sector after the public sector was encouraged to outsource provision in an effort to cut costs. The same period has seen an astronomical rise in the cost of care-home places.[58]

Today, the average cost of a single room in a care home has risen to over £27,000 a year. This is higher than the average UK annual wage (£26,000) and more than double the average annual pension income of £13,208. In fact since 2011, care-home costs have risen at twice the rate of inflation, whilst standards of care have slipped.[59]

Elderly people who have paid for their homes in the hope of leaving an asset for their families have had to sell their homes simply to have their most basic care needs met for the final years of their lives. It is estimated that 40,000 elderly people a year are selling their homes with the aim of covering the average £100,000 care-home costs of the final years of their lives. While the Coalition plans to implement a £75,000 cap on the contributions a person makes to their care-home costs, a) they have stalled the policy until after the next election and b) it won't include accommodation costs, which are the bulk of the issue.[60] This is no help at all.

One might expect that, for these breathtaking sums, the UK would have the finest care homes in the world. Yet in 2012 the regulatory body for the country's care homes, the Care Quality Commission, published a damning report showing that more than half of all the elderly and people with disabilities in care homes were being denied basic care.[61]

People suffering from incontinence were waiting more than two weeks for a consultation on their condition in more than 40 per cent of care homes for the elderly surveyed. One might think that this was a substantial failing, but this was actually classed as success, since 40 per cent of the care homes surveyed set themselves a target of 90 days – three months – to offer a resident this basic check-up.

More worrying still is that the data used for this study only covers 2010, and so does not even take into account the sweeping cuts implemented since. This is the sorry state of care the elderly lived in prior to ideological Austerity.

Some of our old people, moreover, are dying in the most appalling conditions. Take 81-year-old Gloria Foster, who suffered a lonely and excruciating death in 2013 from starvation and thirst, trapped in her own bed, having been left without her essential care for nine days.[62]

The cuts keep coming

In the same week that Gloria Foster lay dying as a result of systemic failures in the care system, Birmingham City Council announced crushing cuts of half a million pounds a year in the budget for providing home care for those like her.[63] Birmingham is not alone. The Mayor of Bristol approved the local council's decision to close 8 of its 11 council-run care homes in January 2013,[64] and in February of the same year two further closures were announced in Peterborough.[65]

In fact, waves of such closures are taking place up and down the country – in Haringey, Anglesey and Maldon, Bute, Ilkeston and Derby – as Austerity drives councils to cut spending on public services despite growing need.

Meanwhile, the private sector is not picking up the slack as promised. There has been an overall drop in care-home places of more than four per cent since the Coalition took office – meaning a little under 1 in every 20 care homes in the UK has closed.[66] Most of this has happened quietly, but there have been notable large-scale closures, such as when care-home company Southern Cross went into administration in 2011. This has largely been blamed on local councils' inability to afford rises in the costs of care, including high rents. However, arguably the bigger problem is that this important service was ever subjected to the ruthless logic of 'market forces' at all.

If we built and owned the care homes, changes in rents would make no impact on care costs as they would be entirely under our purview. If we properly integrated the care of elderly people into our state social-care system, we would not need to meet the rising prices of external providers trying to make ever-increasing profits. If the care of elderly people were a matter for all of us, managed through democratic governance, we could better hold people to account for their failures. Instead, we have abandoned our elderly people to the whims of the free market; they suffer the indignity of not having their most basic care needs met and are bankrupted for the privilege.

Even if elderly people are healthy enough to avoid a nursing home, they face stark choices such as whether to eat, or heat their own homes due to astronomical rises in energy prices.[67] These are people who have worked over 40 years, paid their dues, and often even fought a war on our behalf – for this?

The neoliberal model of privatized, for-profit, core services simply does not work. Any system that views people living longer, healthier lives as some kind of problem is no system worth having. Labour sought and failed to address the problem of profiteering by ramping up the provision of state support, so that taxpayers funded the profits and ameliorated some of the worst effects. The Coalition is simply cutting that support and effectively leaving the elderly to go cold and hungry, and to go more quickly to their deaths. Both these scenarios are ultimately unworkable and undesirable from an economic perspective, let alone a moral one.

1 Gov.uk, nin.tl/1k4IxVs **2** Institute of Fiscal Studies, nin.tl/UGFaXA **3** Gov.uk, 24 Jan 2011, nin.tl/1k4kx3s **4** *The Guardian*, 16 Nov 2011, nin.tl/UGH4rf **5** *The Guardian*, 19 Aug 2010, nin.tl/UGHFcs **6** *The Guardian*, 25 Jan 2013, nin.tl/1k4ml7n **7** *Telegraph*, 2 Mar 2013, nin.tl/UGIrWl **8** *The Observer*, 30 Mar 2013, nin.tl/1k4nbGw **9** Scriptonite Daily, 12 Apr 2013, nin.tl/UGJlT6 **10** *Mirror*, 5 Mar 2013, nin.tl/1k4nMrK **11** Gov.uk, nin.tl/UGK8n7 **12** BBC news, 4 Aug 2011, nin.tl/1k4odT4 **13** *Inside Housing*, 2 Oct 2012, nin.tl/1nR0RkD **14** *Mirror* op cit. **15** *New Statesman*, 21 Jan 2013, nin.tl/1pB4KG4 **16** *The Observer*, op cit. **17** National Housing Federation, nin.tl/1pB6C1l **18** *New Statesman*, op cit. **19** National Housing Federation, op cit. **20** *Inside Housing*, 17 Oct 2012, nin.tl/1nR3PFX **21** *The Guardian*, 25 Jan 2013, nin.tl/1k4ml7n **22** *Mirror*, 27 Jan 2013, nin.tl/1pB9ueB **23** *New Statesman*, 12 Feb 2013, nin.tl/1nR5j2T **24** Ibid. **25** Ibid. **26** Ibid. **27** Ibid. **28** *The Guardian*, 6 Mar 2013, nin.tl/1nR8kAm **29** Gov.uk, nin.tl/1pBeDmW **30** Leighday.co.uk, 30 Jul 2013, nin.tl/1nR9AU7 **31** Channel 4 news, 6 Mar 2013, nin.tl/1pBfMef **32** *York Press*, 2 July 2013, nin.tl/1nkh2rr **33** thefedonline, nin.tl/1nRaFel **34** *Telegraph*, 23 Oct 2012, nin.tl/1pBhoVm **35** Gov.uk, nin.tl/1nRbyDP **36** Huffington Post UK, 28 May 2013, nin.tl/1pBivEJ **37** *Daily Record*, 1 Nov 2012, nin.tl/1nRcgRE **38** Channel 4 news, 26 Sep 2012, nin.tl/1pBjJQc **39** *Liverpool Echo*, 21 Jun 2013, nin.tl/1nRd6xM **40** wowpetition.com/calumn-list **41** *The Guardian*, 31 Jul 2012, nin.tl/1nRdwnO **42** Committee of Public Accounts, nin.tl/1pBlVXY **43** Disabled People Against Cuts, nin.tl/1nRef8z **44** Scriptonite Daily, 25 Jun 2013, nin.tl/1pBneGu

45 *Daily Record*, 24 Jun 2013, nin.tl/1nReTmj **46** *The Guardian*, 17 Oct 2012, nin.tl/1uDS3SV **47** Citizens Advice, nin.tl/1pBvSEN **48** Ibid. **49** Ibid. **50** crisis. org.uk **51** Crisis, nin.tl/1pBz2sd **52** *New Statesman*, 4 Mar 2013, nin.tl/1uDVnxf **53** *Guardian* Letters 25 Mar 2013, nin.tl/1pBB1Nc **54** Kent Online, 1 Mar 2013, nin.tl/1uDWME7 **55** *The Guardian*, 25 Jul 2013, nin.tl/1pBCJOu **56** *The Guardian*, 23 Jul 2010, nin.tl/1uDY4Pz **57** BBC news, 27 Jul 2009, nin.tl/1pBE2wX **58** Allen and Forder; *Competition in the Care Homes Market,* Aug 2011. nin tl/1uDZ9qA **59** This Is Money, 6 Sep 2012, nin.tl/1pBGy6m **60** *Telegraph*, 19 Jan 2013, nin.tl/1uE0i1g **61** *Telegraph*, 7 Mar 2012, nin.tl/1pBI88p **62** *Sutton Guardian*, 5 Feb 2013, nin. tl/1pBKOTp **63** BBC news, 7 Feb 2013, nin.tl/1uE2iGU **64** BBC news Bristol, 4 Jan 2013, nin.tl/1pBLDM4 **65** *Peterborough Telegraph*, 13 Nov 2012, nin.tl/1uE2Ufw **66** Channel 4 news, 14 Nov 2011, nin.tl/1pBMHPZ **67** *The Guardian*, 17 Jan 2010, nin.tl/1k4jYXt

6
Austerity in Britain: some conclusions

UNDER Coalition plans, 'day-to-day spending on public services... [will be at] its smallest share of national income since 1948'.[1]

George Osborne's 2013 Autumn Statement on spending plans for the UK government consisted of 7,025 words and took 50 minutes to read – but could have been summed up by that one line in the report of the government's fiscal watchdog, the Office for Budget Responsibility. This is the purpose of Austerity.

Austerity is ideological

On arrival in government, the dominant Conservative section of the Coalition government was keen to present Austerity as temporary, necessary and purely practical. Back in 2010, Cameron claimed that he 'didn't come into politics to make cuts',[2] and that Austerity was simply temporary spending restraint based on a necessary effort to cut the deficit, not 'some ideological zeal'.[3]

What we can now see, is that Austerity is delivering the half-century-long ambition of the Conservative Party: to revoke the UK's post-War social contract.

The modern welfare state: decent pensions, affordable social housing, a publicly funded and managed healthcare system, a reliable and low-cost transport system, the guarantee of an education regardless of circumstances of birth. This was the social contract the UK public signed up to in the aftermath of the Second World War. Why? Because these generations had lived through the horrific consequences of unrestrained capitalism: enormous inequality; widespread poverty and destitution; starving and malnourished children; an entrenched class system; the benefits of the hard work of the many enjoyed by a privileged and undeserving few.

David Cameron is taking the country back to those dark days. Wearing a white tie, standing at a gilded lectern, speaking to the bankers and brokers of the City of London in late 2013, he stated categorically that Austerity is ideological and would be permanent under a Tory government.[4]

The evidence base for Austerity was dealt a hammer blow in April 2013 by the discovery that the definitive economic paper underpinning it was based on a single Excel spreadsheet with a faulty column. The 2010 'Growth in a Time of Debt' paper was prepared by celebrated Harvard economists Carmen Reinhart and Ken Rogoff.[5] It stipulated that states with a debt-to-GDP ratio of 90 per cent or above grow significantly slower than states with lower debt. They claimed this demonstrated a correlation between debt and growth and that to grow our economies quickly, we needed to prioritize debt reduction. It became the evidence base that political leaders across Europe and North America could use to argue for a dramatic programme of public spending cuts. 'It was not ideological,' they told us, 'it was evidence based.'

George Osborne, speaking in 2010 shortly before he became UK Chancellor, said: 'Perhaps the most significant contribution to our understanding of the origins of the crisis has been made by Professor Ken Rogoff, former chief economist at the IMF, and his co-author, Carmen Reinhart.'

When researchers at the Political Economy Institute of Massachusetts were unable to reproduce the results of the Reinhart/Rogoff study, they requested to review the original calculations. According to *The Guardian*: 'The Massachusetts economists who led the attack on the 2010 paper questioned why their Harvard rivals used a generic Excel spreadsheet to carry out ground-breaking research. According to the European Spreadsheet Risk Group, spreadsheets were behind the collapse of the Jamaican banking system in the late 1990s, and their use was key in the development of collateralized debt obligations – the financial instruments that promised sub-prime mortgages could somehow become AAA-rated investments.'[6]

In their critique of the Reinhart/Rogoff research, the MIT team reported that incorrect formulae in the Harvard spreadsheet meant that the results of the calculations were wrong. On top of this, the spreadsheet omitted data from five of the 19 countries in the study and the wrong data for another. This meant that while the paper claimed countries with a debt-to-GDP ratio on or above 90 per cent would see their economy *shrink* by 0.1 per cent, they would actually *grow* by 2.2 per cent. This is slower than in country with lower debt, but not the doom-laden forecast that triggered the extremities of the Austerity programmes.[7]

It is worth noting that the UK economy has not grown by 2.2 per cent in a single year since the Austerity programme began. Even the architects of Austerity, the IMF, called on the UK Chancellor in 2013 to change direction, arguing that such severe austerity in a time of low growth could only serve to stifle the British economy.[8]

So, how did the UK's political and economic leadership react, when the intellectual basis for the Austerity programme they promoted and implemented was proven bogus, and the results on the ground are so woeful?

There was not a single moment of public pause or reflection. Far from it. They ordered full steam ahead as the ship met the iceberg. Facts don't bother fanatics.

- Mark Carney, the new Governor of the Bank of England, has declared Britain a 'crisis country' alongside the Eurozone and Japan, and argued against the IMF's plea for a U-turn on Austerity.[9]
- Chancellor George Osborne has insisted he will 'stay the course' on Austerity – apparently regardless of the fact that it

puts the majority of the UK population on course for poverty and suffering.[10]

- UK Prime Minister David Cameron seems positively gleeful at the advancement of his Austerity agenda, declaring there is 'no end in sight' for the programme of public-sector cuts.[11]

The UK's political and economic leaders have rejected the evidence that blew, apart the theory behind Austerity, they have dismissed the criticism of the architects of Austerity and they have turned a blind eye to the reality of the programme's devastating results on the ground. These people are not rational, they are ideologues.

Austerity is dangerous

The government provides tax cuts and subsidies to corporations, paid for out of public money that would previously have been spent on public services. In his Autumn Statement of 2013, Chancellor George Osborne promised a 'responsible recovery for all'. Who is he kidding?

While the government continues its assault on the welfare state, and conditions decline for the majority of working and non-working people in the UK, things at the top are only getting better:

Life at the top

- Corporation tax is lower today than at any time in its history. According to data from the Institute for Fiscal Studies, company taxes now constitute only 12.5 per cent (corporation tax is just 7 per cent) of the tax revenues of the UK. In comparison, the people's taxes (income tax and VAT) make up more than 60 per cent of tax income.[12]
- UK corporation tax in 1984 was 52 per cent. By 1986 it was 36 per cent. In 1999 it dropped to 30 per cent. Under the Coalition, corporation tax has been cut from 28 per cent to 20 per cent.

- The top rate of tax has been cut by 5 per cent – this, together with other tax breaks, means that a person earning more than £1 million a year will be saving £107,500 a year.[13]
- Yet in spite of this remarkably reduced tax burden, tax avoidance is costing the UK Treasury almost £70 billion each year.[14]
- Only one in four of the UK's top companies pay their taxes, while they receive tax credits to the tune of hundreds of millions of pounds from public funds provided by people who did pay their taxes.[15]

And what has happened to the nation's debt? According to figures by the Office for National Statistics (ONS) released in August 2013, debt as a percentage of GDP has almost doubled since 2007/8. The ONS report reads:

'Since 2001/02, public-sector net debt has been increasing. At the end of March 2002 net debt was 30 per cent of GDP. Over the next six years, up until 2007/08, the average rate of increase was just over 1 per cent of GDP a year. From 2008 [*at the point of the bank bailout*] public-sector net debt increased sharply, rising from 45 per cent of GDP at the end of March 2009 to 74 per cent of GDP at the end of March 2013.'[16]

Austerity is theft

According to mainstream thinking, the UK is in economic recovery. The economy is now growing again, more people are in employment, and the deficit is shrinking. This is the narrative.

So what's really going on?

The basis of this 'economic growth' is an unsustainable rise in private consumption, which can only be temporary as those consumers are using debt to consume. The government knows this; it is stated clearly in the aforementioned report by the Office of Budget Responsibility. It is temporary, and debt based.

The government has used benefit sanctions to reduce the

numbers of people claiming out-of-work benefits, and used this to argue that more people are in work. The security and dignity of employment has also been diminished. Workfare, zero-hours contracts and other non-jobs mean that while people appear as employed, that employment is neither secure nor adequate to meet their living costs or their aspirations.

This is not an economic recovery by any reasonable definition of the term.

What is the point of GDP growth, if the benefits are not increasing the quality of our lives? The only reason for the public to care about economic growth is the promise that it equates to a better life for us all. Hunger, poverty and homelessness rising exponentially in a time of economic growth can only ever be a political choice. Austerity is planned hunger, planned poverty and planned homelessness. It is the deliberate destitution of the many, to benefit the few.

If the Coalition stays in power or their spending plans are continued (as Labour has all but pledged if it wins the election) to 2018 – it will have taken them just eight years to roll back the UK welfare state 60 years. It is long overdue that compassionate citizens presented a credible and committed resistance to this project. Not only to the present government, but to an entire political and economic system that has enabled corporations to co-opt the parliamentary process, neuter any diversity of political voices, and dismantle the promise of a fair chance for all.

1 OBR, Dec 2013, nin.tl/1kmxUMR **2** *Daily Mail*, 11 Nov 2013, nin.tl/1n3c3Vd **3** *The Guardian*, 12 Nov 2013, nin.tl/1kmyomd **4** Ibid. **5** Carmen Reinhart, Ken Rogoff, 'Growth in a Time of Debt', Jan 2010, nber.org/papers/w15639 **6** *The Guardian*, 18 Apr 2013, nin.tl/1n3eBmj **7** Herdon, Ash, Pollin: 'Does High Public Debt Consistently Stifle Economic Growth? A Critique of Reinhart and Rogoff', Apr 2013. **8** *The Guardian*, 18 Apr 2013, nin.tl/1kmz62N **9** *The Guardian*, 19 Apr 2013, nin.tl/1n3fKdw **10** *The Observer*, 17 Mar 2013, nin.tl/1kmzka8 **11** *Telegraph*, 18 Jul 2012, nin.tl/1n3glMh **12** IFS Briefing Note, nin.tl/1kmzONB **13** *This Is Money*, Nov 2012, nin.tl/1n3icRg **14** *New Statesman* blog, 5 Nov 2011, nin.tl/1kmA3Za **15** *Daily Mail*, 6 Mar 2013, nin.tl/1n3iXKd **16** ONS, nin.tl/1kmBtTm

PART TWO: AUSTERITY AND DEMOCRACY

7
Creating the culture that invites Austerity

AUSTERITY is ripping apart the services, institutions and safety nets that make the UK a social democracy. The concepts of social democracy and the welfare state are anathema to neoliberalism – which knows the price of everything and the value of nothing. Each of the benefits of a welfare state from the social democratic point of view functions as an obstacle to profit-making from a neoliberal viewpoint. So how can the proponents of neoliberalism convince the majority to accept policies that disenfranchise and impoverish them?

In efforts to transform the culture of the UK into one more embracing of neoliberal than of social-democratic ideals, a story has been fabricated that describes anyone who relies on the security of the welfare state as an unaffordable burden or a scrounger. In this way, the culture shift makes attacks on the welfare state that were previously politically impossible not only permissible, but even popular.

Creating the deserving and undeserving poor

Leading members of the UK government have repeatedly taken to the media to publicize the notion of a cultural struggle between strivers and skivers, or the deserving and undeserving poor.[1]

Chancellor George Osborne launched into a false analogy worthy of Nazi propaganda magazine *Der Sturmer* with his speech to the Conservative Party conference in 2012. He asked listeners to imagine a scene in which bedraggled British workers trudged pre-dawn streets on the way to the bus, past houses of benefit claimants slumbering peacefully with their blinds closed. It is the relentless invocation of this kind of imagery that has created a conversation about an over-generous benefits system based on no actual evidence that such conditions exist.

No interview or article on the issue is complete without a question to advocates of the welfare system along the lines of 'but surely it makes sense that the taxpayer only supports the people who really need it?' This is intended to leave the viewer or reader with the following affirmation: because it is right that only the needy should receive support, the government is right to make its changes.

This argument is entirely rhetorical. No-one is suggesting that benefits money should be dropped from the rooftops and enjoyed by all who catch it. Yet any argument against drastic cuts to critical social-security payments is represented as endorsing such a view.

According to the government's own figures, overpayment of benefits due to fraud occurs in just 0.7 per cent of cases, at a cost of £1.1 billion a year. To put this in perspective, overpayment of benefits due to administrative error comes in at almost double this, at 1.3 per cent, or £2.1 billion a year.[2] But we are yet to see government ministers demanding a war on administrative errors at the Department of Work and Pensions.

So it is that 99.3 per cent of people claiming benefits are characterized as if they are suspected of behaving like the 0.7 per cent. The government is deliberately framing the debate in such a way as to distort the issues at hand and to the perception that there is a 'broken benefits system'.

This misdirection is essential to their attempts to transform the culture of the UK and to overturn the post-War consensus of social-democratic principles that would have considered their machinations to be socially and politically unacceptable.

The scapegoating of immigrants

'A banker, a teacher, an immigrant and a politician are sitting at a table, on which rests a plate with ten biscuits on it. While the teacher and the immigrant are deep in conversation, the banker reaches forward and grabs nine of the ten biscuits. He places two of these biscuits in the pocket of the politician.

When the teacher sees there is just one biscuit left on the plate and begins to worry, the politician leans over and whispers: 'Watch out, that immigrant is after your biscuit!"

The scapegoating of immigrants serves two core purposes:

- It creates a popularly accepted decoy reason for the impacts of neoliberal economic policies – rising unemployment, rising wealth inequality, shortages of housing, school places and so on.
- It divides the population, pitting poor against poorer, making a united opposition more difficult to assemble.

The irony is that the working and non-working poor of the UK have far more in common with their immigrant neighbours than with those politicians and pundits stoking their prejudices – which is part of the reason why such stoking occurs.

Net migration to the UK fell by a quarter in 2011/12 from 242,000 to 183,000.[3] This was largely caused by a fall in the number of overseas students choosing to study in the UK (the first such fall in 16 years[4]), and a rise in the number of Britons emigrating (up from 108,000 to 127,000[5]).

Despite this, immigration is once again a major issue for the British people, according to politicians and the mainstream media. It is no surprise that 'the British people' believe immigration to be an issue when so many myths, untruths and outright lies are promulgated by the political class and the mainstream media.

People come to Britain for all sorts of reasons: to take up a place at university; as a result of landing a job; to seek work and better life chances; or to live with a British spouse or family member. People may stay here for a few months, a few years or permanently.

Excluding visitor (tourist) and transit visas, most entry clearance visas are issued under the Points Based System for work. The system breaks up people into labour groups ranked from Tier 1 (highly skilled) to Tier 5 (temporary/unskilled workers).

The numbers of entry clearance visas issued for the purposes of work, study (excluding student visitors) and family reasons have all continued to drop, falling by 4 per cent, 26 per cent and 15 per cent respectively for the year ending September 2012.[6] These points-based visa newcomers account for the vast majority of the UK's immigrant population.

There is another category of immigrant: the asylum-seeker. An asylum-seeker is a person who arrives in the UK as a refugee that has fled their country, and cannot return for fear of persecution or death. Asylum applications constitute just 7 per cent of net migration numbers, with only 33 per cent of applicants granted asylum.[7]

The myth of 'benefit tourism'

The picture overleaf and similar memes have appeared across social media in recent years, generally accompanied by some sort of personal statement like 'I'm not racist but...', or 'We've got to DO SOMETHING about this', and so on.

There has been almost non-stop chatter about 'benefit tourism' of late by various members of the UK government, including Iain Duncan Smith (Secretary of State for Work and Pensions), Jeremy Hunt (Secretary of State for Health) and Prime Minster David Cameron himself.

Whether it's their newspaper, their social media feeds or their political leaders, people cannot move for people telling them that immigration is an issue. It could be argued that this creates, rather than reflects, a pervasive attitude which says that not only are our poor people lazy scroungers, but also now other nations' lazy scrounging poor are on their way, begging bowls at

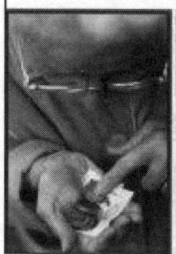 

BRITISH OLD AGED PENSIONER
TOTAL YEARLY BENEFIT £6,000
ILLEGAL IMMIGRANTS / REFUGEES
LIVING IN BRITAIN
TOTAL YEARLY BENEFIT £29,900
The average pensioner has paid taxes
and contributed to the growth of this
country for the last 40 to 60 years.
Sad, isn't it?
Got the guts to copy and paste this?
I Just Did

the ready. An almost unavoidable image has been created of a tsunami of immigrants crashing over UK social services, leaving devastation in its wake.

This is manifestly not the case. Let's bust some myths:

'We're the number one destination for asylum-seekers!'

Asylum claims in the UK are actually well below the EU average.[8]

'We're a soft touch, no-one else accepts this many immigrants!'

Newcomers (immigrants) compose about 9 per cent of the UK population. This is lower than Australia (24 per cent), Germany (13 per cent), the US (12.8 per cent) and France (10 per cent).[9]

'They're all over here for the benefits!'

According to the Department of Work and Pensions' own figures, despite being 9 per cent of the UK population, immigrants make up just 6.4 per cent of the 5.5 million people claiming working-age benefits in the UK.[10] The immigrant community is actually under-represented in the field of benefit claims.

'Immigrants are jumping the queue for council housing!'

A 2009 study by the European Human Rights Council (EHRC), at a time when the Labour government was announcing a crackdown on immigrant access to social housing, proved the fallacious nature of this claim.

The EHRC study found that of newly arrived migrants between 2003 and 2009, including those from Poland and other eastern European countries, more than 60 per cent were living in privately rented accommodation, 18 per cent were owner-occupiers, and only 11 per cent had been allocated social housing. In terms of the overall proportion of new lettings, out of 170,000 new council or housing association tenants in 2006/7 in England, fewer than 5 per cent went to foreign nationals and less than 1 per cent went to east Europeans.

The foreigners are not jumping the queue. Most of them are not even in the queue. One reason for the widespread misconception that they are, is that the vast majority (90 per cent) of housing allocated to immigrants in the private rented sector tends to be former council homes that have been sold off in 'hard to let' (rundown) areas. Their local neighbours may simply assume these properties are still social housing and that the immigrants have been granted it.[11]

The major myths busted, we can now look at the reality of social-security entitlement for people seeking to relocate to the UK.

The majority of immigrants to the UK seeking to claim benefits must go through a Habitual Residency Test. People seeking asylum in this country are forbidden to work while their application is being assessed. It is illegal for them to seek work, no matter how long the claim takes to process. Therefore, unless someone has fled their country with enough cash to live without an income for a significant period of time, they will be forced to rely on hand-outs.

If the applicant is classed as destitute (having no accommodation nor the financial means to pay for it) they can apply for accommodation in dispersal zones across the UK. There is no such accommodation available in London, and spaces are dispensed by the UK Border Agency (UKBA).

Asylum-seekers are not eligible to claim any of the following benefits:

- Income support
- Income-based job seekers' allowance
- Housing benefit
- Council tax benefit
- Social fund
- Disability living allowance
- Attendance allowance
- Invalid care allowance
- Severe disablement allowance
- Non-contributory incapacity benefit
- Working families' tax credit
- Disabled person's tax credit
- Child benefit.

At the time of writing, a single asylum-seeker aged between 16 and 18 receives just £39.80 per week, falling to £36.62 on their 19th birthday. A couple in a marriage or civil partnership receives just £72.52 shared between them. A lone parent is eligible for £43.94 each week.[12]

This compares to a basic state pension (without any personal contributions) of £107.45 per week, or up to £111.45 per week Job Seeker's Allowance. UK nationals would also be able to access the other benefits outlined above, which are not accessible by asylum-seekers.

When one considers how hard it is for people to make do on these sums, as the cost of living rises, it is clear that entitlements for asylum-seekers are, in the first place, nowhere near those of UK nationals and, in the second, not significant enough to suggest a life of indulgence and excess by claimants.

Despite these inconvenient truths, the blame for rising unemployment, poverty and a shortage of housing and school places continues to be heaped upon the immigrant population.

The rise of UKIP

In one of the more absurd twists in this tale, the newest and most popular immigrant-bashing voice is that of the United Kingdom Independence Party (UKIP). This party is seen by a minority of the British public as the alternative to the Westminster élite. It seems to garner votes on two premises – that it will 'do something' about immigration and the European Union, and that it is the only genuine alternative to the mainstream parties.

The first alarm bell that should go off for anyone even considering voting UKIP on the 'alternative' ticket should be the party leader, Nigel Farage. Farage styles himself as a man of the people, but the fact that he drinks pints and chain-smokes says little of the real man. Farage is anything but just 'some bloke down the pub'.

Farage is a millionaire banker, from millionaire banking lineage – his father, Guy Oscar Justus Farage, was a stockbroker.

Farage didn't work his way up from the bottom. He was educated at Dulwich College, a private school that charges £10,000 a term. On leaving college he used his father's contacts to become a commodities trader in the City. A vote for UKIP is a vote to install another wealthy heir in Number 10.

Farage poses as the bloke next door, allowing wine-soaked punters to cry on his shoulder about their concerns. He then takes those concerns and uses them to pit the working classes against each other – the working poor against the non-working poor, the natives against the immigrants. Farage and his party take legitimate rage about bogus Austerity, indistinguishable politicians, and disenchantment with a system that seems to offer little to the average Brit – and he points it away from the source of the problem.

Many who have cast a vote for UKIP know little about its leader, but even less about its policies.

UKIP describes itself as a libertarian party. UKIP, like the Tea Party in the US, seems fundamentally to misunderstand libertarianism. Libertarianism is about the smallest possible amount of government, with a focus on personal liberty and devolved power. Both UKIP and the Tea Party, with their socially conservative attitudes, tend to conceive of personal liberty as extending only to people like them.

- *Immigration*: UKIP would cap net immigration at 50,000 a year, excluding work permits and students. Students (282,833) and work permits (147,385) made up 430,218 of the 2012/13 immigration numbers.[13] That leaves only 78,190. So UKIP are actually talking about reducing immigration by 28,000 people a year. Hardly revolutionary.
- *Gay marriage*: UKIP doesn't have a published policy on Education, but it has one on equal marriage. UKIP opposed the newly passed legislation allowing same-sex couples to marry. They dismissed the entire campaign for equality in the following terms: 'There is, apart from a small but noisy minority within the gay community, no strong demand for this.'
- *Defence*: The UKIP defence policy sounds very much like a conversation down the pub, with about the same level of consideration and evidence base. It says it would disestablish the Ministry of Defence and put decisions of war and peace in the hands of the armed forces – which sounds a little like the foundations of a military state. UKIP politicians rail against the poor terms and conditions of serving and retired members of the armed forces, and rues Britain's declining military power. They make a vast range of promises around replacing Trident with 'a new advanced stealthy cruise-type missile', priority healthcare for forces personnel, and all sorts of new kit, perks and housing, all on the 2010 military budget.

The UKIP policy platform is a messy series of soundbites that lack evidence and are often contradictory – all sound and fury, signifying nothing.

It would be futile to highlight UKIP politicians as homophobic, transphobic or xenophobic – they are omniphobic. They are appalled and terrified about pretty much everything that doesn't look and sound like them. They appeal to the darker angels of human nature which seek out and magnify superficial differences, while overlooking the vastness of our common humanity.

In 2010, the party suspended its Chairman for London, Paul Wiffen, after he made the following racist rant on an internet forum: 'You leftwing scum are all the same, wanting to hand our birthright to Romanian gypsies who beat their wives and children into begging and stealing money they can gamble with, Muslim nutters who want to kill us and put us all under medieval Sharia law, the same Africans who sold their Afro-Caribbean brothers into a slavery that Britain was the first to abolish.'

More recently, UKIP candidates were found to be posting pictures of themselves making Nazi salutes,[14] and one candidate used Photoshop to create a picture of himself standing proudly beside Adolf Hitler.[15] There is also significant crossover in terms of both candidates and supporters from the British National Party (BNP) to UKIP. UKIP is the polite face of the same old 'loathe thy neighbour' politics of hate and envy.

Discussions during 2013 on the UKIP online members' forum on homosexuality and gay marriage were particularly enlightening. Former parliamentary candidate and branch chair for Oxford, Dr Julia Gasper, claimed: 'As for the links between homosexuality and paedophilia, there is so much evidence that even a full-length book could hardly do justice to the subject.' UKIP member Jan Zolyniak posted: 'The evidence is quite clear that the percentage of homosexuals who molest children is very high and cannot be dismissed.' Douglas Denny from the Bognor Regis branch in West Sussex wrote: 'What irritates me is the way they and their leftie, neo-Commie followers seem to want to force the rest of us to consider them as normal.'[16]

A vote for UKIP is a vote for a party of afraid, angry, hateful people. Worse, rather than being an alternative, it actually permits the neoliberal mainstream to push through its policies even more quickly by creating the culture of suspicion, envy and prejudice required. Each vote wasted on UKIP serves to bolster the belief of the most hard-edged neoliberals that the public will accept immigrant bashing, welfare cuts for the poorest and tax cuts for the wealthiest people and corporations.

Cameron's crackdown

The ramblings of the Tory right, and the rise of the proto-fascist UKIP, has gifted prime minister David Cameron with the opportunity to go on the offensive against the *victims* of Austerity rather than be put on the defensive about its *impacts* – and he has fired both barrels at the immigrant population.

Here are the key anti-immigrant measures rolled out so far:

- From 2014, EU immigrants will lose their entitlement to Job Seeker's Allowance after six months' unemployment. This might be a good or a bad idea, but either way it will have very little impact. According to the DWP's own figures, just 6.6 per cent of UK immigrants in 2012/13 were unemployed within six months of receiving their National Insurance number. This compares to 16.6 per cent of British nationals.[17]
- Cameron claims to be taking on 'health tourism' by requiring non-EU nationals to demonstrate that they have health insurance in order to access health services.[18] Dr Kailash Chand of the British Medical Association acknowledges that the unexpected rise in immigration in the mid-2000s did place the NHS under additional stress, yet he also states: 'The rapid rate of immigration is a problem because it was not planned or expected. The resources were not in place. Immigration has caused problems for the health service but with better planning and control it could easily have been avoided.' He goes on: 'The NHS is supported by hundreds of thousands of immigrant doctors and workers. If you removed

them tomorrow the NHS would collapse. They bring a great deal of expertise and the country has not had to pay for their training.'[19] Nevertheless, the attacks continue.

- Secretary of State for Health Jeremy Hunt introduced a new charge for all immigrants of £200 a year to use the NHS. This will apply to students, spouses of British citizens and people who have come here to work.[20]
- The government has also placed a cap on non-EEA (European Economic Area) immigrant workers of 21,700 a year.[21]
- Rules have been tightened on education providers' ability to provide visas for their students, with a number of colleges being stripped of this function. In one such debacle, London's Metropolitan University had its licence revoked, meaning its 2,700 foreign students had just 60 days to leave the country or to apply to another institution in the middle of their studies. It is estimated that these changes will cost the UK £2.4 billion in the next decade in lost tuition fees.[22]
- A UK citizen now has to earn more than £18,600 a year to gain permission to bring a foreign spouse into the country. This is considerably higher than the average annual wage of a waiter (£12,177), a hairdresser (£12,219), a sales assistant (£13,449) or a fishmonger (£15,453).[23] Originally, soldiers were exempted from this legislation, but recent changes mean the armed forces are also impacted by this rule. Given the starting wage for a soldier falls below this figure, what of soldier spouses?

Cameron is contributing to myths that pit dirt-poor UK citizens against dirt-poor newcomers while achieving a negligible real-world result at the very best. It is a political stunt designed to appeal to the fears and prejudices of people that are already being exploited by UKIP. Worse, the Labour Party has now joined in – just to make sure no-one thinks it has an enlightened view on immigration either.

This politics of envy, fear and suspicion is entirely consistent with the kind of 'look over your shoulder' culture that the Coalition government sought to create in the UK. This immigration conversation is intended to sow discord and divert public attention from the true source of their woes – an economic and political system rigged in favour of a fraction of the world's population at the expense of everyone else.

Lessons from history

'First they came for the communists, and I did not speak out –
because I was not a communist;
Then they came for the socialists, and I did not speak out –
because I was not a socialist;
Then they came for the trade unionists, and I did not speak out –
because I was not a trade unionist;
Then they came for the Jews, and I did not speak out –
because I was not a Jew;
Then they came for me --
and there was no-one left to speak out for me.'
Martin Niemöller

Niemöller had been a U-boat commander during the First World War and went on to become a pastor of a wealthy Berlin suburb in 1931. He joined the Nazi Party and was a supporter of Adolf Hitler. He later confessed that Hitler's policies were an extreme reflection of his own prejudices against Communists and Jewish people.

In a 1934 meeting with Hitler, it was made clear to Niemöller that Hitler's next target was the church itself, and that he was under heavy surveillance to ensure his compliance with the transition to the German Christian movement, which introduced the racist policies of the Third Reich into the teachings and practices of formerly protestant churches across the land.

Niemöller became a public critic of Hitler and was arrested by the Gestapo in 1937. He spent the last seven years of the

Third Reich in concentration camps. He wrote the above poem as a reflection on his and others' failure to protect the freedoms and liberties of others, in the mistaken belief that they were somehow superior. Niemöller died in 1994, but his poem lives on – and provides much-needed words of caution that we would be foolish to ignore today.

If we want a window onto the dangerous social consequences of this style of politics, we can look to Greece.

Resurgent fascism in Greece

IMF-imposed austerity measures have reduced Greek society to a shadow of its former self. The resulting unemployment, poverty and homelessness has been hijacked by fascist elements to pit the poor against the poorer. In 2012/13 the Greek government built a series of internment camps and launched raids on immigrant, addict and sex-worker communities. Then they came for the poor and the Lesbian, Gay, Bisexual and Trans (LGBT) people too. Greece can be considered a preview of coming attractions to the UK.

It is worth briefly outlining the socio-economic catastrophe of Greek Austerity.

- In 2010, Greece accepted an £88-billion loan from the IMF and the European Central Bank (and the Austerity measures attached) in order to bail out its banks and stay in the Euro.
- The economy of Greece has shrunk every year for five years and the Austerity programme has turned a financial crisis into a humanitarian crisis.
- Some 11 per cent of the population now live in 'extreme material deprivation' without enough food, heating, electricity or a telephone.[24]
- Unemployment is now over 27 per cent and continues to rise each month, while youth unemployment is now over 59 per cent.[25]
- Unsurprisingly, crime has soared – with burglaries rising by 125 per cent in 2011.[26]

Yet, instead of Austerity itself, it is immigrants who are being blamed.

As the gateway to southern Europe, Greece is a popular destination for immigration. However, with an immigrant population of 10 per cent, Greece is equal to France and lower than Germany (13 per cent), Luxembourg, Cyprus or Malta.[27]

Nevertheless, as poverty levels rise, a resurgent fascist movement spearheaded by the Golden Dawn party has diverted popular rage from the political and economic institutions that eviscerated the Greek economy, onto immigrants – many of whom were simply escaping the previous evisceration of their own economies by those very same institutions.

At the time of writing, Golden Dawn holds 18 of the 300 seats in Greek parliament, and has successfully mobilized a large portion of the Greek population. Its flag contains a swastika-like emblem and in the summer of 2013 it mobilized tens of thousands of Greeks to march through the streets of Athens chanting 'Greece is for Greeks'. They are neo-Nazis, and they are winning.

First they came for the immigrants

The Greek police launched Operation Xenios Zeus in 2012, as part of a crackdown on immigration. This operation, ironically named after the Greek god of hospitality, delivers anything but that to those on Greece's streets who don't 'look Greek'.

In the first seven months of the operation, Greek police arrested more than 85,000 'foreigners' – yet only six per cent were charged with unlawful entry, meaning 94 per cent of these people were lawful residents of Greece.[28] In many cases, those being arrested suffered violent assault by the police in the process and the operation has become nothing more than a means to vilify and bully foreign-looking people.

Tourists to Greece have also been caught up in these arbitrary arrests. In January 2013, a Korean backpacker, Hyun Young Jung, was seized by Greek police as an illegal immigrant, despite showing them his passport and itinerary. When he asked for proof of identity of the police officer arresting him, he was punched in the face.[29]

In the same month, Christian Ukwuorji, an African American travelling on a US passport, was walking through Athens on his holiday when he was seized by police. When he showed police his US passport, they confiscated it and beat him on three separate occasions on the way to the station. His final beating was so severe it left him unconscious – he awoke in hospital with concussion.[30]

Immigrants are also being routinely assaulted and killed in racially motivated attacks. In April 2013, a group of 200 Bangladeshi strawberry pickers protesting six months'unpaid wages were fired upon by their bosses in Western Peloponnese. The shooting left 28 with gunshot wounds and it was a miracle that no-one lost their life.[31]

Further to the sweeping arrests, violence and murder, immigrants are now being rounded up and transferred to internment camps. The first such camps have been openly operating inside Greece's borders since 2012, and more than 5,000 people languish behind their barbed-wire perimeter.[32] The government has announced plans to build 30 more such facilities in the next few years.[33]

While immigrants were the first group to join the ranks of Greece's 'undesirables', they were not the last.

Then they came for the sex workers and the addicts

The next group to face the wrath of the neo-Nazi resurgence were the sex workers and drug addicts.

Greece has previously enjoyed a low prevalence of HIV, but since the economic crisis new infections have skyrocketed; in 2010, the new infection rates shot up by 57 per cent. The blame has been laid at the door of drug addicts and sex workers, but these rises were entirely attributable to the Austerity crisis.

Austerity is driving ever more Greeks to drug abuse while cutting away the social safety nets that would manage and resolve their addiction. In 2010, heroin use grew by 20 per cent.

In areas where the state-funded needle-swap programmes were closed, HIV infections among drug users shot up by 1,450 per cent. As the social security and healthcare systems fail after 40-per-cent budget cuts, some desperate Greek addicts are deliberately infecting themselves with HIV in order to access just $890 of financial support each month and admittance to a drug rehabilitation centre.[34]

Sex work is legal in Greece and largely managed through a ministry of state. However, since the economic crisis began, the sex industry in Greece has expanded by 150 per cent as the least enfranchised Greek women resort to prostitution to make ends meet. There are now a reported 20,000 unregistered, illegal prostitutes on Greece's streets. There has been a rise in sexually transmitted diseases during this time.[35]

Rather than addressing the root causes of these issues, the government has instead demonized the sex workers and drug addicts themselves.

Greek police began raiding brothels and forcing sex workers to undergo HIV tests. In February 2012, the police published the names and photographs of 17 sex workers arrested and testing positive for HIV, branding them a danger to public health. One of the sex workers committed suicide as a result of the public shaming, unable to face her family.

The government has since passed legislation making it legal for police to arrest and detain all suspected illegal sex workers and test them for HIV without their consent. Any woman walking the streets can be arrested on suspicion of illegal prostitution, forced to undergo an HIV test and publicly named and shamed if found to suffer any sexually transmitted diseases.[36]

In this way, the police have extended the tactics used in Operation Xenios Zeus to their treatment of sex workers, drug addicts and the homeless – who have been rounded up and sent off to internment camps with the immigrants.[37]

Then they came for the gays

The Lesbian, Gay, Bisexual and Transgender (LGBT) community

was next to be singled out as 'undesirable' in the new fascist Greece.

The Bishop of Thessaloniki (Greece's second city) came out in strong and public opposition to the city's second Gay Pride festival in June 2013. He denounced Pride as 'an unholy and unnatural event' and garnered 19,500 signatures for a petition calling for the event to be cancelled.[38] The adverts for Pride 2013 across Greece were censored after the inclusion of a lesbian kiss was deemed 'undesirable'. This comes after the October 2012 decision by Greek State TV to censor a kiss between two male characters on *Downton Abbey*.[39]

Things are getting worse rather than better for the gay men, lesbians and bisexual population of Greece, but they have become markedly worse for the transgender community. Greek police are using the sex-worker legislation to target trans people.

The Greek Transgender Support Association reported in summer 2013: 'According to written complaints filed by our members who live in Thessaloniki, it is clear that from 30 May 2013 onwards, the police have been carrying out purges and arrests of transgender citizens on a daily basis. The same complaints state that those arrested are being taken to the police headquarters in Thessaloniki in Dimokratia Square, where the victims are waiting for at least three or four hours to be identified under the pretext that the authorities should establish whether the particular person was not a prostitute.'[40]

The Greek news outlet GR Reporter records:

'The Association stresses that the police behaviour during the arrests was offensive, humiliating and that it was intended to undermine the dignity of transgender persons. In three of the complaints, the victims note that traffic policemen had stopped transgender women while they were driving their cars without any proof or suspicion of any fault or violation of the law. Later, they were taken to the police station in order for their identity to be verified.

'The testimonies of a large number of victims suggest that before being released from custody, the policemen threatened transgender women, warning them that if they did not "return to normal", legal proceedings against them would be initiated for indecent behaviour in public places.'[41]

Then they came for the poor

The full machinery of the Greek state is now being turned on the poor, as they become the newest addition to the 'undesirables'. The Greek parliament is passing legislation to turn a military camp into a prison for poor Greeks.

Since February 2012, any citizen of Greece falling more than 5,000 euros in debt to the state can be imprisoned to work off their debt. The government is now planning to roll this out more systematically, with a specific prison camp dedicated to holding poor Greeks while they work for free for the state.[42] This would conventionally be referred to as a labour camp – the tool of many a totalitarian state, including Stalinist Russia and Nazi Germany.

Coming here soon

We should not only stand against this disintegration of Greek democracy as a matter of principle, but out of sheer self-interest. Greece is just a few years and policies ahead of the UK in the ideological Austerity agenda – and these are the results.

Anyone nursing the mistaken hope that British society is somehow immune to this sort of thing needs to think again. The wave of attacks on mosques and Muslims after the 2013 Woolwich murder of soldier Lee Rigby; a flurry of anti-immigrant legislation; the rise of the UKIP vote; and the rise in hate crime against disabled people: all these point to a society beginning to buckle under the pressure of relentless propaganda blaming 'undesirable elements' for all our ills.

If the UK is resorting to this behaviour, albeit milder than Greece, while unemployment is below eight per cent, the health service remains free at the point of use, and schools and community services are still open – how is it going to be once Austerity enters its next phase and all of these go south? Well – that is down to you and me. It will be a choice. People will either keep their heads, and keep their eyes on the systemic issues that create poverty, or they will scapegoat whomsoever the state decides to brand as 'undesirable'. The power over that choice always remains with the citizen.

1 *Metro*, 16 Apr 2012, nin.tl/1umEnlc **2** Department for Work and Pensions, nin.tl/1mueRRx **3** BBC news, 29 Nov 2012, nin.tl/1swbAkY **4** *Huffington Post*, 11 Jan 2013, nin.tl/1umGXhi **5** BBC news, op cit. **6** Office for National Statistics, nin.tl/1sweztJ **7** Migration Observatory, nin.tl/1swfqdO **8** Ibid. **9** Shelter factsheet, nin.tl/1umlZhq **10** Gov.uk Jan 2012, nin.tl/1swpDaf **11** *The Guardian*, 29 Jun 2009, nin.tl/1umOdtA **12** Gov.uk, nin.tl/1swriN1 **13** BBC news, 30 Aug 2012, nin.tl/1swt68P; Gov.uk, nin.tl/1umRgSl **14** *London Loves Business*, 30 Apr 2013, nin.tl/1umTuRQ **15** *Anorak*, 1 May 2013, nin.tl/1swx3u4 **16** *Mirror*, 12 Jan 2013, nin.tl/1umV1Y6 **17** Channel 4 news, 25 Mar 2013. nin.tl/1swy3hL **18** *The Sun*, 26 Mar 2013, nin.tl/1umX3rb **19** *Mirror*, 18 Oct 2007, nin.tl/1swz7SK **20** Channel 4 news, 3 July 2013, nin.tl/1umYkhT **21** BBC news, 14 Apr 2011, nin.tl/1swAf9d **22** *The Guardian*, 5 June 2013, nin.tl/1umZ0UA **23** *The Guardian*, 25 Nov 2011, nin.tl/1swBhBS **24** *Counterpunch*, 26 Feb 2013, nin.tl/1swBULN **25** zerohedge.com nin.tl/1un1x0R **26** *The Guardian*, 29 Mar 2012, nin.tl/1swDgWT **27** Eurostat, nin.tl/1un2al2 **28** *openDemocracy*, 9 Jul 2013, nin.tl/1swEi5a **29** *The Guardian*, 10 Jan 2013, nin.tl/1un33Ag **30** *Washington Post*, 10 Jan 2013, nin.tl/1swFndq **31** *The Independent*, 18 Apr 2013, nin.tl/1un3Q41 **32** keeptalkinggreece.com nin.tl/1swGFow **33** *The Guardian*, 29 Mar 2012, nin.tl/1swDgWT **34** *The Fix*, 21 Jun 2012, nin.tl/1swHKNl **35** *EnetEnglish*, 23 May 2013, nin.tl/1un5Rxb **36** Ibid. **37** seriouslyepicstuff.com nin.tl/1swJiXq **38** *Greek Reporter*, 31 May 2013, nin.tl/1un6R4y **39** radiobubble.gr 17 May 2013, nin.tl/1swKt9A **40** GRReporter, 4 Jun 2013, nin.tl/1un7Otq **41** Ibid. **42** keeptalkinggreece.com nin.tl/1swGFow

8

The rise of corporate fascism

'The first truth is that the liberty of a democracy is not safe if the people tolerate the growth of private power to a point where it becomes stronger than their democratic state itself. That, in its essence, is Fascism – ownership of government by an individual, by a group, or by any other controlling private power.'

Franklin D Roosevelt, message to US Congress, 29 April 1938

IT is ironic that the economic system Roosevelt's representatives went on to pioneer at the Bretton Woods conference in 1944, in the final stages of defeating one fascism, would write the roadmap to drive the nations of Europe, Africa, Asia and North America right back there within a few generations. Neoliberalism and the Austerity project are placing governments in the hands of controlling private power.

What's fascist about Blighty?

Using Roosevelt's definition, no doubt examples are already coming to your mind. I am choosing deliberately to reference contemporary examples so as to underscore the proximity and urgency of the situation, and to avoid the debate becoming lost in the fog of chronological distance.

When you look at the bank bailout, the Health & Social Care Bill, the Welfare Reform Bill, workfare, the privatization of the police force and the education system, it is easy to spot a common thread: the transfer of public services to powerful private interests, funded by public money.

Now, in conventional economics there are a couple of principles that purport to make the market free. For the sake of expediency, I am not going to challenge these assumptions here.

- **The best 'man' wins**: A business (a person or organization providing a product or service to other persons/organizations in return for remuneration) prospers when its product or services beat those of its competitors at attracting customers. These customers have free choice over the suppliers in the market, and choose based solely on their idea of best value.
- **Moral hazard**: In the event that a business fails to achieve the above, to such a degree that it is no longer financially viable, it fails. The company is dissolved, made bankrupt or diversifies. If a company or individual is allowed to take risks without being the one responsible for the consequences, then moral hazard becomes an issue. They are likely to take unacceptable risks, as if they win they keep the profit, but if they lose they do not take a hit.

It is clear to see that collusion between big business and the UK parliament in recent years has rendered these two rules obsolete. This is how.

Best 'man' wins? A customer compelled

Libertarians would argue that all compulsory tax is theft. The idea that a government can compel an individual, through fear of sanction, to hand over money they have earned themselves has those of a libertarian viewpoint ill at ease from the get-go. However, even if one agrees with a compulsory taxation system, it is easy to see that in a fascist context, this principle, which one might normally look upon as beneficent, can become fraudulent in practice.

For example, let's say I want to buy a vacuum cleaner. (Let's leave out all those factors that complicate the analogy like comparative advantage and fair trade; let's say we live in Adam Smith Land where the market is free.) I can scour the market for the vacuum cleaner that most meets my requirements in terms of functionality, appearance, cost, quality and so on. Even after all that, I can buy any one I like, or none. All this is done entirely by my own free will.

By contrast, the Health and Social Care Act, the academization of schools and the privatization of police stations put private, profit-making providers in charge of public services. The services, although free at the point of use, are paid for through a tax I have no choice over paying, unless I accept legal or other sanction. In the past, this tax was agreed on the basis that it was a communal pool of funding for a public service, delivered by public employees, accountable to a parliamentary representative.

The changes mean that money given in good faith is diverted from that agreed course, to create new markets and revenues for private interests, with private employees who are neither accountable to the state nor, by extension, to me. This makes me, you, all of us, legally obliged customers of Virgin, G4S, Serco, Circle, and any other corporation to which the government flogs off our services.

What is worse is that these companies have failed to attract most of us out of the state model. Most of us use the NHS rather than private healthcare, most of us use the state education system rather than private education, most of us wouldn't consider using private security over calling the police. Unhappy with their market share, these corporations have succeeded, through the collaboration with a parliamentary system that is increasingly inseparable from the corporate world, in cheating the rule of the market. They don't need us to choose them – the choice has been made for us and we are simply compelled to hand over our taxpayer cash.

There is no mainstream party that does not espouse these 'neoliberal' policies, which means that utilizing the vote to arrest this process is not possible. This egregious domination of our democracy by self-serving corporatism is fascist.

Moral hazard

To recap: according to the National Audit Office, UK National Debt rose by £850 billion as a result of the bank bailout. This is almost twice the nation's total annual budget. For this amount, the UK could have funded the entire NHS for **8 years**, our whole education system for **20 years** or provided **200 years** of Job Seeker's Allowance.[1]

Despite current propaganda that the national debt and the ensuing Austerity policies are required to roll back excesses in public spending, the reality is that the financial crisis was caused by the unregulated financial services sector.

Most of the individual traders responsible for the crash are still at work trading in the same dodgy derivatives that created the crisis. The derivatives market is still unregulated and continues to accumulate a further pile of toxic debt which will one day implode again. This currently stands at $700 trillion[2] – nearly ten times the annual earning power of the entire planet ($77 trillion[3]).

But beyond the individual traders are the leaders of the banks, the people responsible for the strategy and the system that rewarded unacceptable risk-taking and greed. Did they at least face culpability for their crimes?

Goldman Sachs – Hank Paulson

Goldman Sachs played a key role in the crisis, making huge profits in the derivatives trades that busted the global financial system. The CEO at the time of this egregious behaviour was one Hank Paulson. Mr Paulson oversaw the sale of dodgy derivatives to pension firms, local governments and other misinformed investors. The bank also, appearing to foresee the crisis, sold more than $3 billion in collateralized debt obligations in the first half of 2006, immediately betting against them.[4] That same year, Paulson left to become Treasury Secretary of the US and, in doing so, was able to sell his Goldman shares without paying capital gains tax. He made $485 million. If he had held onto the stocks, they would have been worth just $278 million.[5] In his new position, Paulson leads meetings with world leaders and has become the chief architect of a taxpayer-funded bailout of the crash he helped create.

Paulson now sits on a personal fortune estimated at over $700 million,[6] is a senior fellow in the University of California's Harris School of Public Policy and is still an opinion former on the economics world stage.

Meanwhile, Goldman Sachs dished out £8.3 billion in bonuses in 2012/13, working out at an average £250,000 a year for each employee.[7] This is higher than the pre-crash bonus pool in 2007.[8]

RBS - Fred Goodwin

On 7 October 2008, the Royal Bank of Scotland, the world's largest bank (measured by assets), failed. The UK government chose to inject £45.5 billion of public money into the bank to prevent its total collapse.

The Financial Services Authority report on the collapse blamed the bank's failure on 'underlying deficiencies in RBS management governance and culture which made it prone to make poor decisions'.[9]

The RBS story makes incredible reading. It is simply a litany of greed-driven dodgy trades to maximize short-term profits at the expense of ordinary bank employees and the taxpayer.

For his role in the scandal, CEO Fred Goodwin was stripped of his knighthood, got a few weeks' bad press and saw his RBS pension reduced from £650,000 a year to £342,500 a year.[10] RBS employees, meanwhile, who saw their pensions and share savings wiped out by the bank's failure, could be left with as little as the basic state pension of £5,727 a year.

RBS continues to break the law. In February 2013, RBS received a £390-million fine for rigging the LIBOR rate (the rate of interest at which banks lend money to each other in London). UK and US regulators found rigging of the rate was 'widespread', involved 'a number of employees and occurred over a number of years'. The scheme aimed to make money by using interest-rate swaps to bet on interest rates the traders had already rigged.

RBS has also been using interest-rate swaps to bankrupt small businesses, then buy their devalued assets and sell them on at a profit.

The small businesses were told they could only receive a loan from the bank if they took out an interest-rate swap, which, the bank advised, would act as a hedge, protecting the customer from future rises in interest rates. The swaps were sold to the customers as a mandatory insurance policy, protecting customer and bank from future risk. In reality, as interest rates were being kept artificially low as a matter of UK economic and monetary policy (something the banks were well aware of) these swaps actually involved small businesses making vastly higher interest payments – more money for the bank. Furthermore, the bank registered small businesses with swaps as higher-risk customers, and charged them a higher rate of interest on the loan – yet more money for the bank.

Finally, as the small businesses struggled to finance their loans, the bank would force a crisis (by demanding settlement in an impossible timescale, or refusing further credit), seize the assets of the destroyed business, and then use a subsidiary arm to buy up the properties at knockdown prices and sell them on at a profit.

Property developer Chris Kashourides told Channel 4 News that, after his property was seized by RBS in 2010, another arm of the bank called West Register bought the property at auction for £415,000. Just four months later, it sold the same property for £1,000,000. Mr Kashourides was forced to sell 25 more of his properties after RBS suddenly gave him just seven days to pay off his overdraft in 2010, or face the seizure of his assets.[11]

In July 2013, RBS was fined £5.6 million for failing to report accurately (or at all) more than a third of its wholesale transactions. This means many of the financial transactions on assets such as shares, government bonds and derivatives (like those interest-rate swaps!) between RBS and other firms went unreported or misreported – making it impossible for the regulator to assess whether these trades were lawful.

In November 2013, the RBS pot of compensation for having mis-sold Payment Protection Insurance (PPI) to customers reached £2.6 billion.[12] PPI was originally intended to provide loan repayment cover in the event that customers became sick or lost their job. However, bank employees were encouraged to sell PPI to customers who didn't need it. In many cases, customers did not know what they were buying, and in the worst, were signed up to the costly scheme without their knowledge.

In December 2013, the European authorities fined RBS £324 million for having rigged the LIBOR rates of Europe (Euribor) and Japan (Yen LIBOR).

In the same month, RBS received a $100-million fine from US regulators for violating sanctions against Iran. RBS removed information from sanction-busting trades with Iran in order deliberately to conceal what they knew to be criminal actions. Between 2005 and 2009, more than 3,500 of these illegal transactions were made, totalling more than £523 million.[13]

RBS has engaged persistently in criminal activity on an industrial scale over the better part of a decade. This behaviour has continued unabated, despite bringing the 300-year-old institution to its knees in 2008, to be saved only by a costly taxpayer-funded bailout.

The sanction-busting, PPI-mis-selling, small business-bankrupting, LIBOR-rigging, transaction-hiding corporate criminals at RBS face no personal criminal censure for their crimes. In each case, the punishment has been an easily repayable fine to the corporation, while the individuals retain personal fortunes amassed from the proceeds of crime.

HBOS – James Crosby

According to findings of the Parliamentary Commission on Banking Standards, way back in January 2004, the Financial Services Authority (FSA) and the HBOS Board were told by Group Finance

Director Mike Ellis that 'the Group's growth had outpaced the ability to control risks. The Group's strong growth, which was markedly different than the position of the peer group, may have given rise to "an accident waiting to happen".'[14]

Around the same time, HBOS's own internal Head of Group Regulatory Risk Charles Moore raised his concerns to the Board: that HBOS was growing too quickly and its internal controls of Risk, Compliance and Finance were inadequate to manage this growth safely. Moore found himself summarily dismissed by HBOS Chief Executive James Crosby. Moore used whistleblowing procedures to sue for unfair dismissal in 2005, won substantial damages from HBOS and received a gagging order.[15] Crosby denied the claims and was supported by both the FSA and then Prime Minister Gordon Brown.[16]

Both the FSA and the HBOS board ignored these warnings, and in 2007 the 'accident' happened – the bank crashed. The allegations of Moore were proved entirely accurate.

The UK government injected £8.5 billion in taxpayer money into HBOS but this was not enough. HBOS needed to be taken over by Lloyds TSB to survive and received a further £12 billion from the taxpayer as part of the deal.

According to the damning verdict of the Parliamentary Commission on Banking Standards' Fourth Report: 'the FSA's regulation of HBOS was thoroughly inadequate.' The report states that the FSA's focus moved away from HBOS after 2004, and even after HBOS collapsed the regulator took more than five years to launch an investigation into the bust bank.[17]

In a stunning coincidence, HBOS chief executive James Crosby was appointed to the Board of the FSA in 2004. He became Deputy Chair of the FSA in 2007, just as HBOS was crashing. Although RBS didn't fold until a year later, the FSA put HBOS at the back of the queue for investigation.

Crosby has since been enjoying a non-executive directorship for catering company Compass worth £125,000 a year and an HBOS pension of £580,000 a year, alongside other lucrative positions with MoneyBarn and Bridgepoint.

Despite being found responsible for the failure of HBOS, the loss of £20 billion of public money to save it, the summary dismissal of the Head of Group Regulatory Risk for doing his job, and the conflict of interest between his roles at HBOS and the FSA, Crosby has yet to face a courtroom. As Liberal Democrat Business Secretary Vince Cable began to make press-pleasing sabre rattles over instigating a 'City Ban', barring the likes of Crosby from leading Financial Services companies again – David Cameron signalled his lack of interest in becoming actively involved.

In a bid to provide the essential blood-letting that would allow ultimate inaction (like Goodwin before him) Crosby offered up his knighthood (for services to banking) and just 30 per cent of his £25-million pension pot, leaving him to struggle by on £406,000 a year. He resigned his Bridgepoint directorship but maintains his other positions and is free to pick up others worth more than £125,000 a year. All talk of a City Ban has evaporated.[18]

What does it take for a banker to go to jail?

One Goldman Sachs banker did go to jail. Rajat Gupta was sentenced to two years in October 2012 for insider trading. He was jailed for, as the judge in his case put it: 'stabbing Goldman in the back'.

Yes, he was jailed for losing Goldman Sachs money.

Gupta received letters from Kofi Annan and Bill Gates requesting leniency in his case. The judge stated in his sentencing order: 'The Court can say without exaggeration that it has never encountered a defendant whose prior history suggests such an extraordinary devotion, not only to humanity writ large, but also to individual human beings in their times of need.'[19]

Despite this, Gupta's behaviour in providing a tip that lost Goldman cash was considered worthy of an example-making custodial sentence of two years, and a $5-million personal fine.

The US Attorney in Manhattan (where the trial took place),

Preet Bharara, told the *Wall Street Journal*: 'Violating clear and sacrosanct duties of confidentiality, Mr Gupta illegally provided a virtual open line into the boardroom for his benefactor and business partner, Raj Rajaratnam.'[20]

There are some mind-boggling double standards in operation here. When acting as Chief Secretary to the US Treasury, Hank Paulson, former Goldman Sachs chief executive, tipped off a room full of hedge fund managers (five of whom were alumni of Goldman Sachs) that US mortgage giant Fannie Mae was to receive a government bailout.[21]

He spent previous and subsequent days and weeks assuring the press and public outside the room that Fannie Mae would not receive a government bailout. On 13 July he stated: 'If you have a bazooka, and people know you have it, you're not likely to take it out.'

On 21 July, he proceeded to reveal to the hedge fund managers, in detail, his plans to bail out Fannie Mae. This amounts to insider trading – the sharing of non-public information with those who could financially gain from such knowledge. How is this any different from the behaviour of Gupta? Except in the case of Paulson, the ramifications were far greater.

'You just never ever do that as a government regulator – transmit non-public market information to market participants...There were no legitimate reasons for those disclosures.' So said William Black, a former general counsel at the Federal Home Loan Bank of San Francisco, and Associate Professor of Economics and Law at the University of Missouri.

Janet Tavakoli, founder of Chicago-based financial consulting firm Tavakoli Structured Finance Inc, was even more blunt. 'What is this but crony capitalism?' she asks. 'Most people have had their fill of it.'[22]

The lesson here is: bankers go to jail when they defraud banks, not when they defraud the public purse.

For defrauding the taxpayer, and wrecking whole national economies, not one banker went to court or jail. Not one new regulation has been placed on the financial derivatives market.

These same products are being packaged and sold across the financial services industry right now. The banks were left free to carry on with business as usual, on our tab.

Instead of this prompting criticism of big business, despite the 'banker bashing' which we often hear condemned in the media, it's the state system which has been lambasted and ripped apart. The economic crisis went from being a corporate failure to a public-services failure.

The neoliberal solutions?

- Greater deregulation of markets, especially the financial-services industry which has been recast as the greatest wealth creator rather than the greatest debtor.
- A violent contraction of the welfare state, and a blanket condemnation of those unfortunate enough to find themselves without work due to ill physical or mental health, disability or sheer lack of jobs.
- Finally, private enterprise must take a leading role in the provision of public services… because they are more efficient than the current public providers of, apparently, any service. Schools, hospitals, police forces, the welfare system: all of them opened to private providers paid for by the public purse.

In short, the neoliberals have turned a crisis into an opportunity – an opportunity to extend the reaches of corporate power, using the structural power of the state to enforce it.

Rising fascism in the UK

In his 1995 essay, 'Eternal Fascism', Italian thinker and essayist Umberto Eco provided one of the most compelling and 'eternal' definitions of fascism available to date.[23] He set out the key characteristics observable in a fascist state. He did not specify that all these conditions needed to exist for the state to be defined as fascist, but that all of them are indicators of a fascist disposition. Such conditions are being created in UK society.

Fear of difference

As stated previously, the neoliberal-dominated institutions of politics, media and even economics have made strident efforts to rebrand the Financial Crisis – a clear crisis of the private sector and neoliberalism itself – into a public-sector crisis. This scapegoating has affected a number of groups, but through 2013, it was the narrative on immigration that was ratcheted up out of all proportion to the size of the issue.

Constant media and political attention is expended on the immigration issue – with almost no time asking the question – why are people coming here? Many migrants are economic migrants, and those who are not are political migrants – both are systemic, not personal issues. To argue in favour of 'closing the door' on people fleeing the system our country is so pivotal in exporting around the globe, often by force – what kind of morality is this? This is the national equivalent of the first-class passengers guiding their lifeboats away from the steerage passengers after the sinking of the Titanic. The problem is the sinking ship, not the poor bastards swimming for their lives.

In July 2013, the UK government launched the 'Go Home' campaign.[24] This consisted of driving vans around predominantly poor, mixed-ethnicity areas of London with a billboard warning immigrants of serious consequences for overstaying illegally, and a text number to report illegal immigrants.

Some might ask – how is this racist? It is racist because it contributes to the total lie that immigration is out of control and to a culture of fear and suspicion of people who look different from the majority – 'any of them could be an illegal!'

In the same week, in the same areas, UK Border Agency officers wearing stab vests patrolled commuter hubs such as Kensal Rise, Stratford and Walthamstow train stations stopping predominantly non-white travellers and asking them to produce credentials proving their right to be in the country. Reports suggest that these officers became aggressive when questioned as to what right they had to request this information by those being stopped and by concerned passers-by. This might well be because under UK law the police do not have the right to perform random ID checks such as this without direct cause for suspicion – they are not permitted to perform this kind of random stop and search using racial profiling techniques. This is because a person in the UK should not be suspected of being an illegal immigrant because they look or sound 'foreign' to a police officer or anybody else. It is the painful memory of the yellow stars and the pink and black triangles that singled out Jewish, gay and disabled people during the Third Reich that serves to underpin this protection in law.

Finally, the UK Home Office Twitter account took to producing statistics each day of how many 'suspected' illegal immigrants they had arrested under the hash tag #immigrationoffenders – even displaying pictures of people they had arrested (even though they were still only 'suspects') for the public to gawk and point at.[25]

The fact that people are still even asking 'how is this racist?' speaks to just how damaging this conversation about immigration has become. The UK population is being taught to fear the 'illegal' and the 'immigrant' as a drain on their resources, while the country is actually being feasted upon by privateers and profiteers. Immigration, fear of difference, is being used as a decoy – diverting justified anger into safe (from the point of view of the one per cent) channels.

Contempt for the weak

To be clear, we are talking here about the neoliberal interpretation of 'weak'. This is someone who is unable to perform the primary role of a citizen under this system by serving as a resource with which to generate profit.

One of the most absurd aspects of the current system is that there is so much work to be done, so many people who could contribute to that work, and yet people are only permitted to earn a living through 'jobs'. These jobs may not match a person's skills, or deliver the most critical work that needs doing. Furthermore, we do not make the most efficient use of people to deliver maximum utility for their effort because of things like the physical layout of the workplace, inflexible hours and the penalization of sickness absence.

In short, we do the wrong things, in the wrong way, with half our team on the bench – and then we blame the people left behind rather than the system. This isn't just an ideological problem, but a problem that destroys and ends lives.

Secretary of State for Work and Pensions Iain Duncan Smith and Tory Party chair Grant Shapps have repeatedly misrepresented data on benefit claims and the results of their policies. The made-up figures made it into press releases, which resulted in bogus articles in the *Telegraph*, the *Mail*, *The Sun*, the *Express* and the ITV and BBC news (along with myriad local news outlets) – all of which parroted the misinformation without bothering to verify it.[26]

Lies repeated often enough become the truth and a climate of suspicion forms around those who find themselves reliant on the welfare system.

The cult of tradition and rejection of modernism

The cult of tradition is the premise that all that is knowable is already discovered and it is for us to accept this rather than seeking to define some new idea.

While the public are encouraged to become embracers of the modern in terms of technological and scientific progress, when it comes to new ideas for organizing ourselves socially, politically and economically – the cult of tradition and the rejection of modernism is wheeled out to shut down and stifle debate.

In a 2013 piece for my blog *Scriptonite Daily*, I charted the emergence of the idea that There Is No Alternative to neoliberal capitalism. This idea was launched and embedded under Margaret Thatcher, but entirely embraced by New Labour (hence the 'New'), the Conservative Party and the Liberal Democrats.

The ultimate mendaciousness of the cult of tradition, though, is that it presents itself as modernism. It hijacks the language of progress. Words such as 'reform', 'modernize' and 'develop' only apply if referring to neoliberal change to an organization, institution or economy. Anyone suggesting that this might not be the most effective, efficient or ethical way of running things is treated not as a critical thinker, but as a heretic.

The cult of tradition in neoliberalism is so powerful that even people who consider themselves 'apolitical' find themselves regurgitating embedded verbal memes to close down others who are attempting to think their way out of it. Memes like 'well, what do you want, Communism?! That worked well in Russia!' or the idea that talking 'politics' is somehow dry, boring or oppressive.

Economics professor Steve Keen has described the ideological cleansing of universities in the field of economics, such that students are only taught neoliberal theories and only academics endorsing the neoliberal view receive research grants or publication in major journals.[27]

Perhaps part of the reason this rising corporate fascism appears unthreatening to much of the population – if it is even recognized – is that it seems to be the province of politicians or academics. There has been a failure, to date, fully to communicate the real-life, daily impacts of corporate fascism. That is our next task here.

1 *Guardian* datablog nin.tl/1odW7QW **2** Managing Partner, nin.tl/1kp52DF **3** Earth Policy Institute, 2011, nin.tl/1pZah9n **4** Charles Ferguson, *Predator Nation*, Crown Business, New York, 2013. **5** Bloomberg, 7 Jan 2009, nin.tl/1kp5Ic2 **6** Richest Net Worth nin.tl/1pZaPfx **7** *The Guardian*, 16 Jan 2013, nin.tl/1kp6e9Z **8** Bloomberg, 18 Dec 2007, nin.tl/1pZbgXj **9** *Telegraph*, 12 Dec 2011, nin.tl/1kp6Wnw **10** BBC news, 31 Jan 2009, nin.tl/1pZbKws **11** Channel 4 news, 13 Oct 2013, nin.tl/1kp7nOJ **12** *International Times*, 1 Nov 2013, nin.tl/1kp7Ct7 **13** BBC news, 11 Dec 2013, nin.tl/1pZcCkU **14** Parliamentary Commission on Banking Standards, nin.tl/1pZcPoc **15** BBC news, 10 Feb 2009, nin.tl/1kp8vlt **16** BBC news, 11 Feb 2009 nin.tl/1pZd8zl **17** Parliamentary Commission on Banking Standards, nin.tl/1pZcPoc **18** *The Guardian*, 9 April 2013, nin.tl/1kp9aTW **19** *Huffington Post*, 24 Oct 2012, nin.tl/1kp9yBW **20** *Huffington Post*, 15 Jun 2012, nin.tl/1pZecDg **21** Bloomberg, 29 Nov 2011, nin.tl/1kpa5nx **22** Ibid. **23** Umberto Eco, 'UR-Fascism', *New York Review of Books*, 1995. **24** *The Guardian*, 29 Jul 2013, nin.tl/1pZeKZP **25** nin.tl/1kpcyhD **26** *The Guardian*, 15 Apr 2013, nin.tl/1kpd0MX **27** Steve Keen, *Debunking Economics*, Zed, London, 2011.

9
Attacking employment rights

THERE appears to be a pervasive illusion in Western democracies that the reason their labour is not exploited like that of workers in 'developing' nations is because our corporations or governments are somehow more 'developed'.

This illusion is dangerous, as the rights that protect us from such exploitation are being withdrawn. Yet the vast majority of British (or global) working people are not fighting to retain them in the false belief that times have changed and that any suggestion of a return to past conditions is baseless scaremongering.

In reality, we would all still be suffering these conditions today, were it not for the relentless efforts of collectivized bargaining by unions of workers past. Each protection in law was won by workers, not gifted to workers. They were not the trickle-down benefits *of* capitalism. They were won *from* capitalism.

Busting the unions

The rights to unionize, bargain for pay and conditions collectively, and withdraw labour through strike: this co-operative approach to holding corporate power to account brought workers rising wages, reduced hours, the concept of work-life balance, the weekend, health and safety in the workplace, and an end to the slave-like conditions working people endured through the 18th, 19th and early 20th century.

Successive governments of Heath, Thatcher, Major, Blair and Cameron have pitched their war against the unions as if the unions were something other than working people – while simultaneously creating conditions for unions to become bloated, bureaucratic policers of dissent among working people.

Between 1980 and 1993, there were six Acts of Parliament to curtail collective power through unions. These included:

- **Outlawing secondary action or 'sympathy strikes'**. The upshot of this was that workers could not lawfully strike in solidarity with an abuse of workers' rights elsewhere in the economy.
- **Ballots and notifications**. The Trade Union Act of 1884 required unions to hold a ballot and notify the government of the results ahead of any industrial action. In 1993, it was made mandatory for these ballots to be postal and unions were compelled to provide seven days' notice of a strike. All this served to raise the cost and bureaucracy of unionizing. It put an end to workers being able to surprise employers and government alike with flying pickets, and other unannounced industrial actions. It also placed the union executive in ultimate charge of the process, whereas before workers could create pressure for a strike from the bottom up.
- **Injunctions**. Employers were granted powers to apply for High Court injunctions to prevent industrial actions where the legality was in doubt. This was made all the easier by the 1993 Trade Union Reform and Employment Rights Act, which added a new level of complicated procedural compliance. Prior to this legislation, debate about the legality of a strike was based on substance – the trade dispute itself. Since this reform, corporate lawyers have been able to gain or threaten injunctions against unions not on the basis of merit, but by utilizing the Kafka-esque complexities of notifications, reporting and subconditions of subclauses.[1]

The list continues well beyond these few examples. The unions were neutered. In 1970, employers lost 10 million days of labour through industrial action.[2] In 2012 – in the midst of consistent real-terms wage cuts, reduced pensions, extended working hours, reduced job security and other impacts on working people – just 250,000 days were lost to industrial action.[3] This is nowhere near the kind of impact that holds corporate (and corporatized state) power in check. As a result, at a time when the UK has the fastest-growing economy in the West, its people also have the fastest falling wages.[4] And the consequences do not stop there.

In Victorian Britain, those unlucky enough to form the ranks of the newly unemployed amid the process of industrialization and urbanization were placed in workhouses. In return for shelter and food, they were required to work as many hours as the authorities dictated. Sadly, a century and a half on, workers in the UK are heading back into the workhouse conditions their predecessors fought so hard to escape.

Jobs without pay

Unemployed people in the UK seeking work at their local Job Centres have been appalled to find that the jobs being advertised are not actually jobs, but workfare placements. Below are a sample of adverts at Job Centres captured and reported to Ipswich Campaign for Unemployed Rights[5]:

Job Title: CLEANING PRINCIPLES PATHWAY
Hours: 16 hrs p/week over 5 weeks
Wage: N/A
Description: A comprehensive training package for entry into cleaning roles in offices, schools, hospitals and factories. Course consists of a Level 2 Award in Cleaning Principles, awareness of COSHH, identifying risks in the workplace and preparation for entry into work.

Job Title: CLEANING OPERATIVE
Hours: 16 hrs week, 5 days from 7
Wage: Benefits plus expenses
Description: Experience preferred but not essential as full training will be given, good communication skills are essential as you will be expected to liaise with our clients. Duties will include general cleaning, vacuuming, mopping and cleaning toilets of domestic, industrial and office locations. The successful applicant will need a full UK driving licence as they will be required to travel around various sites in the North West. Work trial only.

Job Title: CLEANING OPERATIVE
Hours: 30 per week over 5 days
Wage: JSA Continuation
Description: This is a Work Experience opportunity. You should be able to clean to a high standard and be flexible, reliable and thorough. Duties include different stages of cleaning new build houses in preparation for handover to clients and tenants.
A driving licence and previous experience in using scrubber dryers and carpet cleaning equipment would be advantageous. This could lead to permanent employment.

Jobs without hours

Employers in the UK are increasingly employing staff on 'Zero Hours' contracts. These contracts have no specified working hours – meaning that an employee is placed on permanent standby until the employer needs them. While classed as employed, the person has no wage security as they cannot guarantee their pay from one week to the next.

The Labour Force Survey of 2005 showed that 11 per cent of employers in the UK were operating these schemes. By 2011 that figure had more than doubled to 23 per cent.[6] This means almost a quarter of all employers are utilizing this exploitative method of retaining labour. In July 2013, it was revealed that 307,000 workers are on zero-hours contracts in the social-care sector alone.[7]

The Resolution Foundation – UK Think Tank of the Year 2013 – published a review of zero-hours contracts that same year that detected serious problems with this employment model:

- Those on zero-hours contracts earn less than half the average wage (£236 compared with £482 per week) of those on proper contracts.
- Workplaces using zero-hours contracts have a higher proportion of staff on low pay (within £1.25 of the minimum wage) than those who do not.[8]

These factors have allowed the UK labour market in recent years to combine a relatively high level of employment and an unprecedented squeeze on wages.

- Those on zero-hours contracts work 10 hours a week less, on average, than those who are not (21 hours compared with 31 hours).
- 18 per cent of those on zero-hours contracts are seeking alternative employment or more hours compared with 7 per cent of those in ordinary contracts.[9]

These factors have contributed to the rise in underemployment in the UK since 2008. A government survey last year revealed that more than a million people had been added to the ranks of the underemployed since the 2008 bailout of the banks.[10]

- Zero-hours contracts are hitting young people the hardest, with 37 per cent of those on such contracts aged between 16 and 24.
- Zero-hours contracts are more likely to be held by those without a degree, and with a GCSE as their highest level of education.
- Non-UK nationals are 15-per-cent more likely to be employed on such a contract than UK nationals.[11]

It is not difficult to see the advantages of zero-hours contracts to employers – they can achieve maximum flexibility, effectively retaining their workforce on a pay-as-you-go basis. It is also clear that, in the short term, the government of the day also enjoys the advantage of hiding the true effects of their cut-throat economic policies. But the ordinary human being seeking to meet the rising cost of living is losing on all counts.

Jobs without rights

In October 2012, Chancellor George Osborne unveiled his plan that workers could choose to forfeit their remaining employment rights in return for shares in their employer.[12]

This is a most cynical manipulation. Successive governments have contrived to force worker wages below the cost of living, and the current government is now capitalizing on this by having workers surrender their remaining rights in order to receive a much-needed short-term financial benefit in their pay packet. But in the medium and longer term? The door would be open to zero job security, no unfair dismissal cases, no restrictions on hours, no minimum wages, and no protection from unhealthy or dangerous working conditions.

Liberal Democrat Business Secretary Vince Cable has already introduced limitations to workers' rights that will dramatically reduce job security and protection from exploitative or dangerous working conditions. The Enterprise and Regulatory Reform Act (passed in April 2013) brings forward a series of changes that will make it easier to sack employees and harder for them to fight back. One section of the Act reduces potential compensation to those found to have been unfairly dismissed by an employer – previously capped at £74,200. The Act introduced a cap of 12 months' pay or £74,200 (whichever is lower) – meaning those with a lower wage will receive much less in compensation. Worse still, the legislation includes provisions to reduce the cap further to just £25,882 in future.[13]

When disgraced Barclays banker Bob Diamond was forced to resign in the wake of the LIBOR rigging scandal, he left with a year's worth of perks including use of a company car and chauffeur, private medical insurance, life insurance cover, accommodation while in Britain and tax advice. He also received a two-million-pound pay day in July 2013.[14]

In the UK today, corporate criminals receive greater dismissal payments than regular working people who have been mistreated by their employers. But it doesn't stop there.

The Act halves the period of consultation required when a company is to sack more than 100 people, from 90 to just 45 days. This would mean employees in a small to medium-sized firm could receive little more than a month's notice of collective dismissal.

The Act also makes the employee pay to go to Tribunal. These costs have historically been passed to the employer or the state, for obvious reasons. In cases of unfair dismissal, discrimination or whistleblowing, the plaintiff in the case (not the defendant corporation/organization) will face costs of £250 to apply and £950 for a hearing. At appeal, they will face a £400 flat fee to lodge their appeal and £1200 for the hearing (more than the monthly wage of half the UK population).

Perhaps the most cynical piece of the Act, though, relates to the permission of employers to have 'protected conversations'. This means an employer can take a staff member aside without prior warning, offer to pay them to leave the firm, make comments on their performance and the employee will be unable to use this conversation or any record of it in (non-discriminatory) tribunal proceedings.

The assault on wages

The net result of three decades of so-called 'liberalization' of employment protections has been a devastating reduction in wages. Increased access to personal debt (credit cards, loans, store cards, buy now pay later, hire purchase and so on) has been masking the expanding gulf between the cost of living and the level of wages for decades.

In the 10 years between 1999 and 2009, the average annual salary rose by 13.6 per cent. During the same period, house prices went up 130 per cent, a loaf of bread went up 147 per cent, and a litre of petrol went up 42 per cent.[15] This goes some way to accounting for the fact that personal debt rose during this period by 158 per cent.

In the period of Austerity between 2008 and 2013, wages increased by just 10 per cent. The UK Essentials Index, which focuses on the kinds of everyday items bought by the UK's working and non-working poor, showed an inflation rate of 33 per cent during the same period.[16] This means that the poorest working people's wages are worth 20 per cent less than they were back in 2008. And it's getting worse.

In the UK today, the cost of living is rising at four times the rate of wages. As we have seen, UK wages are falling faster than any other 'developed' country. As a result, the three most expensive benefit payments in the UK are not 'out of work' benefits. Around 65 per cent of the total spent on working-age benefits is actually going to people in work. Tax credits, housing benefit and child benefit, totalling £56.4 billion a year,[17] have been effectively set up for the taxpayer to subsidize poverty wages.

Instead of challenging the disparity between wages in our economic system, the Coalition government perpetuates the war on wages for the lowest paid. The government has even begun claiming that the minimum wage should be frozen or cut if it presents a danger to the UK economy, or business.[18] Both parties in the UK's coalition government campaigned against the introduction of the minimum wage for UK workers in 1998 (the Liberal Democrats eventually and begrudgingly supporting the proposal). They were united in their view that by its very existence, the minimum wage presented a danger to the economy. At the time, Vince Cable, the current Business Secretary, called the policy 'misconceived' and suggested it set a 'dangerous precedent'.[19] Many sections of industry have argued against the minimum wage since its inception, and argued against rises in line with inflation every year since. Once again, this is a set of politicians and corporations making economic policy based on self-interest and ideology, not the public interest.

It is yet more alarming when you realize that it is not just working people in the UK who are having their wages undermined, but workers around the world.

In the US, the earnings of so called 'high-school drop-outs' have fallen 66 per cent since 1969, and people with some college education – the median education level in the US – have seen their wages drop by a third.[20]

The trend in rising global wages has almost stopped. Wages rose 3 per cent in 2007 and have dropped each year since to just 1.2 per cent in 2011 (0.2 per cent, if you remove China from calculations).[21]

Contrary to the language of 'workers versus shirkers' in the UK, working people are working harder than they ever have, and for less.

Research by the International Labour Organization shows that rises in labour productivity have outstripped wage inflation at an ever-increasing rate in recent decades. Between 1999 and 2011 labour productivity (the output of workers' time and efforts) increased at double the rate of wages.[22]

Commentators of the neoliberal persuasion cheer on this assault on wages as a sacrifice that has helped the UK and those other countries employing such tactics avoid the ravages of unemployment enjoyed by European states such as Greece, Italy, Spain or Portugal. Yet it seems the people forced to make the largest sacrifices are the people least able to afford to do so. The same executives cutting their employees' wages in the name of Austerity were simultaneously approving inflation-busting pay rises for themselves. The average pay of executives in the FTSE 100 rose an average of 12 per cent in 2011 alone (more than the average wage rose in the previous decade), with 25 companies boosting executive pay by 41 per cent.[23]

Not only are average wages rising more slowly than inflation, but the incomes of the top one per cent of earners are rising significantly faster than inflation, creating an ever bigger wealth gap. US income inequality is at its greatest for nearly a century and is rising, as the income gap between the bottom 90 per cent and top 1 per cent of Americans reaches its largest since 1928. When compared globally, the US is the second most economically unequal society (behind Chile).

Income inequalities within a developed country result in radically skewed life outcomes, including poorer health, and vastly reduced social mobility. And this is in spite of the fact that once a nation reaches the absolute economic development of the OECD countries, the income differentials between countries do not amount to much. It is absolutely the economic inequality within a country such as the US, not how rich that country is overall, that dictates the quality of life for the majority.

According to research by the University of California at Berkeley, 1928 saw the top one per cent of Americans receive 23.9 per cent of all pre-tax income, and the bottom 90 per cent get 50.7 per cent. By 1944, the impacts of redistributive efforts such as Roosevelt's New Deal, had seen this gap close dramatically: the share of the top one per cent had fallen to 11.3 per cent and the bottom 90 per cent had seen their share of income grow to 67.5 per cent. The gap continued to close until the late 1970s, with the increasing gap since returning the US to 1928 levels this year.[24] So what changed?

Primarily, the ascendance of neoliberal economic policies put forward by the likes of US neoliberal economist Milton Friedman and the Chicago School, who considered redistributive policies and other state interference in markets as a barrier to, not a bringer of, equality.[25] Friedman once wrote: 'A society that puts equality – in the sense of equality of outcome – ahead of freedom will end up with neither equality nor freedom... On the other hand, a society that puts freedom first will, as a happy by-product, end up with both greater freedom and greater equality.'[26]

Friedman was wrong. Economic inequality matters, because inequality of income translates to inequality of outcome.

The UC Berkeley research supports the view that Friedman's assertion was incorrect. This point is underscored by the evidence of economic inequality produced by the Organization for Economic Cooperation and Development (OECD). What is particularly useful about the OECD data is that it compares countries before and after redistributive policies such as taxes are applied.

In the case of the US, the gap in absolute income compares favourably with other developed countries – the US being 10th most unequal. But after accounting for taxes and transfers, the US rises to become the second most unequal society. Conversely, Ireland begins with the largest gap in incomes, yet applies redistributive policies to render it the 10th most unequal.

As Friedman argued that freedom was synonymous with equality of outcomes, not incomes – his point might still stand, except that inequality of incomes can be shown to equate to inequality of outcomes.

In *The Spirit Level*, epidemiology experts Richard Wilkinson and Kate Pickett chart data that proves societies that are more equal are healthier and happier. By comparing life expectancy, mortality rates and other health indicators, Wilkinson and Pickett demonstrate a correlation between inequality of income and inequality of health outcomes.[27]

The study, and a replication of its findings by the Joseph Rowntree Foundation,[28] characterizes those outcomes as an inequality in life expectancy, rate of death and overall physical and mental health. Additional indicators of quality of life and social mobility, highlighted in both papers, were unequal outcomes in educational attainment, likelihood of conviction and incarceration for crimes, and an array of others, which might point to a causal link between income inequality and inequality of outcomes.

Proving such a causal link is notoriously fraught with complexities and uncertainties. However, several studies have sought to assess the independent impact of inequality on health and social problems. One such study suggested that loss of life as a direct result of the impacts of income inequality in the US during 1990 was equal to the combined loss of life due to lung cancer, diabetes, motor vehicle accidents, HIV-related causes, suicide and homicide.[29]

Economic inequality is also hereditary; a social inheritance passed from parent to child. Research by Gregory Clark of the University of California found data to suggest that in the same time period that neoliberal economic policies expanded the economic inequality gap, the rate of social mobility (increased incomes and outcomes by successive generations) declined for the first time in 1,000 years.[30]

For Americans, and citizens across the world, outside the economic élite, rising economic inequality means rising inequality of health and wellbeing; and their inherited disadvantage is proving a barrier to improving not only *their* circumstances, but those of generations to come.

Neoliberalism's basic assumption, of equality as a by-product of dismantling protections from the whims and travails of this cartel-based system, has been proven false. Yet none of the mainstream political parties or successive governments have sought to develop a solution to the inherent problem of perpetually falling wages, regardless of the economic conditions. New Labour identified the combined problem of falling wages and rising living costs and sought to balance the two through increasing 'in work' benefits. The Coalition government identifies a problem of excessive benefit bills and reduces eligibility for and generosity of said benefits. Both scenarios are ultimately unsustainable.

1 Industrial Law Journal, nin.tl/1sFb4kH **2** National Archives, nin.tl/1uvJu92 **3** Office for National Statistics, nin.tl/1sFbEPi **4** CNN Money, 6 Mar 2013, nin.tl/1uvKwlt **5** Ipswich Unemployed Action, nin.tl/1sFcQ5I **6** *The Guardian*,

4 Jul 2013, nin.tl/1uvLoX4 **7** *The Independent*, 4 Jul 2013, nin.tl/1sFe5Bt **8** Resolution Foundation, nin.tl/1uvN2rM **9** Ibid. **10** Office for National Statistics, nin.tl/1sFeW5k **11** Resolution Foundation, op cit. **12** *The Guardian*, 8 Oct 2012, nin.tl/1uvO1rZ **13** *The Guardian*, 23 Mar 2013, nin.tl/1sFfNmk **14** CNBC, 8 Mar 2013, nin.tl/1sFgoVp **15** This Is Money, nin.tl/1sFhdgW **16** Tullett Prebon Research, nin.tl/1uvQltz **17** BBC news, 29 Oct 2010, nin.tl/1sFid4E **18** *Telegraph*, 1 Apr 2013, nin.tl/1uvRzdV **19** Labour List, nin.tl/1sFiPqP **20** *Washington Post*, 31 Jul 2012, nin.tl/1uvSc78 **21** ILO, nin.tl/1sFjmci **22** Ibid. **23** *The Guardian*, 11 Jun 2012, nin.tl/1uvTaQE **24** Pew Research Center, nin.tl/1sFkj4m **25** Julio H Cole, Universidad Francisco Marroquin, nin.tl/1uvU53B **26** Milton and Rose D Friedman, *Free to Choose*, Harcourt Brace Jovanovich, New York, 1980, p 148. **27** Richard Wilkinson and Kate Pickett, *The Spirit Level: Why Equality is Better for Everyone*, Penguin, London. **28** Joseph Rowntree Foundation, nin.tl/1sFm6X3 **29** Lynch, J, P Due, C Muntaner, et al, 'Social capital – is it a good investment strategy for public health?' Journal of Epidemiology & Community Health, 54, 1998, pp 404-8. **30** UC Davis, nin.tl/1uvWFa1

10
Outsourcing the justice system

'Law and order exist for the purpose of establishing justice and when they fail in this purpose they become the dangerously structured dams that block the flow of social progress.'

Martin Luther King Jr, Letter from Birmingham City Jail[1]

OVER the last four decades, the services and institutions of law and justice in the UK have increasingly been taken out of the hands of representative government and consigned to corporate control. This chapter will detail what was sold, whom it was sold to and when. The next chapter on civil liberties and human rights will detail the natural consequences of this behaviour – a justice system tilted in favour of protecting the interests of those who own it.

Throughout the Thatcher, Blair and Coalition governments, there has been a continued trend of outsourcing the justice system. Where, previously, public-sector employees delivered a service for the public, now private companies aiming to make a profit have replaced them. One of the biggest benefactors of the largesse of the UK state has been security giant G4S.

The G4S empire

In 1992, G4S became the first private contractor to run a state prison – taking over HM Prison Wolds. Since then, G4S has been allowed, by successive governments, quietly to buy up large tracts of our formerly public police, security and justice sector.

It is increasingly likely that if someone commits a crime in the UK they will be arrested by a G4S-provided officer and detained in a G4S cell. They may then be transported in a G4S van to a court staffed by G4S security officers. They could subsequently be sent to a G4S prison before being released into the G4S probation service to live in a G4S-run halfway house.

G4S currently enjoys more than one billion pounds' worth of contracts with the UK government. The Ministry of Justice, the Department of Work and Pensions, the Department of Health, the Department of Education, the Ministry of Defence and the Foreign Office all contract out services to the company.

The reach of the G4S criminal-justice empire is eye watering.

- *Policing* G4S has been expanding its control of the police service since the mid-1990s and now manages: 30 custody suites; 500 cells; large portions of the forensic service; and a national database of 30,000 former police officers and staff contracted back to cover resourcing gaps.
- *Prison and detention* Since the early 1990s, governments have contracted out the building and management of prisons to the private sector. At present, there are 14 such prisons out of 139 in the UK.[2] G4S runs six of these,[3] including HMP Altcourse, which was the country's first Private Finance Initiative (PFI)prison, yielding even greater profits for G4S.[4] The company also pioneered the 'Working Prison'[5] where inmates work a 40-hour week for next to nothing for private corporations such as the engineering firm, Norpro.[6]
- *Court services* G4S runs prison transport services and security within court buildings.
- *Electronic monitoring* The company currently monitors 40,000 people in the UK every day. It provides electronic tagging, voice verification and satellite tracking on behalf of the Ministry of Justice and the UK Border Agency. It also designs and builds monitoring services and sells them back to government.[7]

- **Immigration and borders** G4S runs two 'immigration removal centres' – these are effectively prisons in which to hold migrant families and individuals ahead of deportation. The firm also controls two regions of the Border Agency's COMPASS contract to provide accommodation for immigrants/asylum-seekers.[8]
- **Children's services** Three purpose-built 'secure training centres' are managed on behalf of the Youth Justice Board.[9] G4S also has seven specially designed residential homes for children with severe emotional and behavioural problems.
- **Sexual assault support centres** The government has commissioned G4S to run two support centres supporting victims of rape and sexual attacks in the West Midlands. G4S-trained crisis workers will operate the support centres, conduct medical assessments and make recommendations for further action and support required by the victim.[10]

G4S is now focusing on gaining more lucrative PFI contracts to build new prisons, as the government has announced the closure of seven existing prisons. The firm has also built up a new 'offender rehabilitation team' to make use of the government's decision to privatize the Probation Service almost completely. The government has announced that it will put 70 per cent of the service out to competitive tender – while banning the existing Probation Service from competing for the contracts.[11]

Last year, the public-owned Probation Service met or exceeded all its performance targets – with victim feedback positive in 98 per cent of cases – and in 2011 the service received the British Quality Foundation's Gold Medal. This is a public service at the top of its game. Yet its functions are being transferred to companies like G4S, whose performance history suggests our government is putting its ideological commitment to privatization above its duty of care to the public.

One might be forgiven for concluding that, given the ever-increasing portion of the UK justice system surrendered to the control of G4S, the company must be delivering outstanding results. However, this conclusion could not be further from the truth.

The failures of G4S

The case for outsourcing these services to G4S always follows the same logic: efficiency, modernization, higher-quality services at a lower cost. Yet this is rarely, if ever, what the taxpayer receives once the ink has dried on the contracts. Here are just a few examples of the failings of G4S in the fulfilment of its public-services contracts.

Olympic inadequacy

G4S won the £284-million contract to provide security for the London 2012 Games In March 2011. Later, the government was forced to call in the armed forces to do this job after G4S announced a huge shortfall in the required staff numbers just weeks before the event.[12]

The death of Jimmy Mubenga

Jimmy Mubenga, who was 46 years old, was deported by G4S guards in October 2011, yet before the plane had even left the tarmac at Heathrow he was dead.[13] Twenty-one passengers and crew on the plane reported hearing Mubenga repeatedly cry for help and that he could not breathe while several G4S guards applied aggressive methods of restraint – including pressing his head down below the level of the tray on the back of the seat opposite for 10 minutes, a technique known to carry a risk of asphyxiation. Paramedics were called after Mubenga stopped breathing and he was pronounced dead at the scene.

Stuart Tribelnig, the officer in charge of Mubenga's deportation, was a former heavy goods driver who became a deportation custody officer for G4S after a four-week training course in 2007. While on trial, he was made to read out a string of racist jokes that he had texted to fellow G4S deportation guards.[14]

The Home Office's initial response was to castigate the doctors and lawyers who had brought the allegations to light, accusing them of 'seeking to damage the reputation of our contractors'.[15]

Overcharging for electronic tagging

Ministry of Justice spending on electronic tagging has soared from the original £107-million contract offered to G4S to the £700 million paid to G4S and Serco in 2012.[16] Both firms pulled out of the bidding for new electronic tagging services contracts in early 2013 when the Serious Fraud Office revealed that it was opening a criminal investigation into alleged mass overcharging on the existing contract.[17]

The National Audit Office (NAO) published its report on the matter in November 2013, revealing overcharging on an industrial scale.[18] The private security firms had been charging for services never rendered, for the same work several times over, and for long periods (years) after electronic tagging had ceased. Highlights include:

- G4S billed the taxpayer £4,700 for monitoring an offender even though the equipment had been removed 935 days earlier.
- Serco had been unable to install equipment at a criminal's address but carried on charging for almost five years, at a cost of £15,500.
- A criminal was handed four separate court orders for four offences, leading Serco to bill the taxpayer four times 'rather than one charge for the subject'.
- G4S charged for 612 days' tagging – at a cost of £3,000 – even though it had been informed that the offender had been sent to prison and the company had removed the monitoring equipment from his home.

G4S has offered the government £24.1 million in credit notes – an offer the government has rejected, while an audit reveals the true figure of the fiasco.[19]

If you or I were caught stealing £24, we would face criminal prosecution. Yet, a corporation like G4S can 'overcharge' £24 million and get off with an apology and handing back the proceeds of its misdeeds. On what planet is this considered a just system?

Slum housing for asylum-seekers

In 2011, G4S was awarded a £620-million government contract to provide housing for asylum-seekers. G4S subcontracted this out to a network of smaller firms, and the results were disastrous. A 2013 Parliamentary Inquiry found that the firms had repeatedly failed to provide housing fit for human habitation. Shadow immigration minister Chris Bryant described the 'hideous conditions' in asylum housing.[20]

Almost every service that G4S has been given to run has ended up costing us more, whether that is measured in pounds sterling or in human suffering. Yet the UK government seems determined to hand over ever more of the nation's most critical public services into this company's unworthy hands. Despite a litany of performance failures, malpractice and outright fraud, the G4S gravy train continues to roll.

G4S is just one of the companies seeking private profit from the criminal-justice system. And even if G4S, Serco et al were as efficient and ethical as we might wish them to be, the example of the US suggests that there might be a major problem with a privatized model that means more criminals in the system means more profit.

The US injustice system

The US has the highest incarceration rate in the world. This means that a higher percentage of US citizens pass through the prison system than in any other country on the planet.

For most countries demographically comparable to the US, there are around 100 prisoners per 100,000 population. In the US, the rate is five times this at 500 per 100,000.

However, black men in the US are incarcerated at an

astonishing rate of 3,074 per 100,000.[21] This is not because black men are somehow genetically more predisposed to crime, but is thanks in large part to what the American Civil Liberties Union (ACLU) calls the 'school to prison pipeline'.

The average prisoner has been educated only to 10th grade and about 70 per cent have not completed high school.[22]

The ACLU describes a 'disturbing national trend wherein children are funnelled out of public schools and into the juvenile and criminal justice systems. Many of these children have learning disabilities or histories of poverty, abuse or neglect, and would benefit from additional educational and counselling services. Instead, they are isolated, punished and pushed out. "Zero-tolerance" policies criminalize minor infractions of school rules, while high-stakes testing programs encourage educators to push out low-performing students to improve their schools' overall test scores. Students of color are especially vulnerable to push-out trends and the discriminatory application of discipline.'[23]

The school to prison pipeline starts with underfunded public schools. The schools are generally overcrowded and lack the money to pay for the qualified teachers, counsellors, special educational needs resources and even textbooks that they need. The children are clear from the get-go that their education is not being invested in – and these schools are normally in disadvantaged areas in the first place. Hope and aspiration are in short supply.

The implementation of 'zero tolerance' policies in schools has turned minor infractions into criminal offences. This saw suspensions rise from 1.7 million in 1974 to 3.1 million in 2001 – with a disproportionate impact on non-white children.[24]

A combination of major under-resourcing and fear of school-based shootings has seen an influx of police into schools. Instead of teachers, many US schools now have 'school resource officers' (police officers) patrolling the hallways, criminalizing standard misbehaviour. Again, 'children of colour' were disproportionately represented in the statistics – making up

70 per cent of school arrests made.[25] So, what were these children arrested for?

- In Fairfax County, Washington, six-year-old Salecia Johnson was handcuffed, charged with battery and placed in a holding cell for throwing a tantrum.[26]
- In Texas, 12-year-old Sarah Bustamantes was arrested for spraying herself with perfume in a bid to stop bullies picking on her and saying she was smelly.[27]
- In Albuquerque, a 13-year-old boy was handcuffed and hauled off to juvenile detention for burping in class.[28]
- A high-school student had her arm broken by a school security guard after she left crumbs on the floor having dropped some birthday cake in the cafeteria. She was then arrested for littering.[29]
- In San Francisco, a seven-year-old student with special educational needs was pepper-sprayed in the face by a police officer for climbing onto a bookshelf in school.[30]

In 2011, the New York Police Department arrested more than one student a day in the public school system, and 90 per cent of those were black.[31] And in 2010 the state of Texas issued 300,000 'Class C Misdemeanour' tickets to US schoolchildren as young as six – resulting in fines, community service and even prison time.[32]

Instead of children being educated about positive and negative behaviour, they are being criminalized from an early age. Their education is being suspended or ended due to these punishments and they are gifted to the prison system.

The truth is that disadvantaged children in the US have become a source of profit for the private prison industry. Over the past four decades that private prisons were rolled out across the US, there has been an explosion in crime.[33] Did US citizens suddenly become more criminal? No. Rather, poverty was criminalized from the school system onwards.

The Corrections Corporation of America (CCA) is the largest private prison provider in the country. A June 2013 report by US justice organization Grassroots Leadership found the following:

'CCA has made profits from, and at times contributed to, the expansion of tough-on-crime and anti-immigrant policies that have driven prison expansion.'

The multi-billion-dollar corporation oversees more than 65 correctional and detention facilities, containing more than 90,000 beds in 19 states and the District of Columbia. Its record of prisoner abuse, poor pay and benefits to employees, scandals, escapes, riots and lawsuits is long and sad.

In response, faith denominations, civil rights groups, criminal justice reform organizations, and immigrant rights advocates have repeatedly argued that the profit motive creates perverse incentives for prison and immigrant detention systems to keep incarceration rates high.

In short – it pays to lock people up.

Whether through its controversial economic and political ties, or its operational cost-cutting and prison labour practices, CCA is living testimony that the *modus operandi* of the for-profit prison industry is at odds with civic goals of reducing incarceration rates and raising standards in correctional facilities.

This is what happens when the profit motive is introduced to the justice system. A justice system working in the public interest seeks to reduce crime as a social disorder, whereas one working for profit views crime as a source of income. An outsourced justice system seeks to deliver criminals, not justice.

The demise of Legal Aid

Back in the UK, poor people attempting to seek justice are finding it all the harder, as the Legal Aid budget is cut. Legal Aid is taxpayer-funded financial support provided to people for a range of legal services, including:

- advice on your rights and options and help with negotiating;

- someone speaking on your behalf at court without formally representing you;
- help or mediation outside court in a family dispute after your relationship has broken down;
- representation at court by a solicitor or barrister;
- representation at tribunal proceedings such as those to do with mental health, asylum or immigration.

The UK government has chosen to cut £220 million from Legal Aid provision, which amounts to slashing the one-billion-pound budget by almost a quarter.[34] The cut is combined with punitive changes to eligibility and other rules. Michael Turner QC, head of the Criminal Bar Association, said: 'Make no bones about it, we are facing devastation to what is the finest legal system in the world.'[35]

The government is cutting the number of contracts given to firms for Legal Aid from 1,600 to just 400, and putting these out to competitive tender. This is likely to see contracts awarded to low-cost, low-quality, law mega-shops like those run by Tesco, G4S and even haulier Eddie Stobart. Law bodies argue that this will deny those reliant on Legal Aid specialist legal advice and representation, adversely impacting disabled people, those with poor mental health and asylum groups. The process is also likely to result in the closure of more than 1,500 high-street solicitors. In September 2013 the renowned Tooks Chambers, whose lead QC Michael Mansfield represented the families of Stephen Lawrence, Jean Charles de Menezes and Dodi Al Fayed, announced that it was winding up as a direct result of the Legal Aid cuts.[36]

The government is also removing the right for a person to choose their own solicitor – anyone reliant on Legal Aid will have a legal representative appointed by the state, which may well mean the lowest-cost option is chosen, regardless of the needs of the user.

These low-cost law firms will be paid exactly the same fee whether the client pleads guilty early or protests their innocence, creating a longer, more complex case. This creates an incentive for legal representatives to encourage an early guilty plea from their Legal Aid clients.[37]

A new residency test is being applied that will bar those with 'little or no connection to this country' from Legal Aid support for civil cases. The Catholic Church has condemned this change as harmful to victims of human trafficking and domestic abuse.[38]

In a quite astounding move, the state will also remove eligibility for Legal Aid for any judicial Review where it deems the likelihood of success to be less than 50 per cent.[39] Quite how this can be estimated is anyone's guess. Judicial reviews are currently used to great effect by disabled people and victims of workfare to challenge the government's welfare reforms. In future, such cases could become impossible as the state (the proposed defendant in the case) will have the power to deny them funding.

The Law Society, which represents more than 120,000 solicitors, is willing to sue the government over these planned changes to Legal Aid, which it says are 'so unworkable and damaging that they are likely to push the justice system beyond breaking point to a devastating collapse'. Law Society President Lucy Scott-Moncrieff said: 'The removal of client choice is a red line. We believe, on the advice of leading counsel, that it is unlawful... Combined with the cut in fees, the potential impact on the quality of justice in this country is profound.'[40]

The tax cut gifted to the richest in the land in the 2013/14 budget will cost the Treasury three billion pounds a year.[41] This is three times the cost of the entire Legal Aid budget. There is public money enough to provide tax cuts for the wealthiest, yet not enough to provide justice for the poorest. These are not essential cuts, they are choices.

There exists a neoliberal consensus in the parliamentary, academic and media institutions of the UK that makes it almost impossible peaceably to oppose the status quo. The justice system is the one institution left with any claim to independence, and that too has been utterly compromised – it is being rapidly re-engineered to ensure that those suffering at the bottom are left with no lawful means of opposing their ever-worsening conditions.

1 African Studies Center, University of Pennsylvania, nin.tl/1AbAFV5 **2** politics. co.uk, nin.tl/1AbBwEY **3** G4S UK, nin.tl/1sSFFvi **4** HMP Altcourse, nin.tl/1AbChOD **5** G4S UK, nin.tl/1sSGOD4 **6** Corporate Watch, nin.tl/1AbCPUx **7** G4S UK, nin.tl/1sSHEjd **8** G4S UK, nin.tl/1AbDuWb **9** G4S UK, nin.tl/1sSIkFb **10** *Birmingham Mail*, 23 May 2013, nin.tl/1AbEh9s **11** Harry Fletcher, *Comment Is Free*, 9 Jan 2013, nin.tl/1sSJ794 **12** *Telegraph*, 21 May 2013, nin.tl/Y5ODKC **13** *The Guardian*, 16 May 2013, nin.tl/1u8yJtA **14** *The Guardian*, 15 May 2013, nin.tl/Y5PrPD **15** Clare Sambrook, *Our Kingdom*, nin.tl/1xoWLSS **16** *Telegraph*, 17 May 2013, nin.tl/Y5Q63J **17** *Telegraph*, 6 Aug 2013, nin.tl/1u8CKOK; Serious Fraud Office, nin.tl/Y5QUFF **18** National Audit Office, nin.tl/1u8EuaE **19** *Telegraph*, 9 Nov 2013, nin.tl/Y5RJ1f **20** Clare Sambrook, 'Another G4S scandal', 19 Mar 2013, nin.tl/1u8GaRs **21** Population Reference Bureau, Aug 2012, nin.tl/Y5TOdB **22** Ibid. **23** ACLU, nin.tl/1u8Noow **24** Ibid. **25** Dignity In Schools, nin.tl/Y5VUu3 **26** *Washington Post*, 18 Apr 2012, nin.tl/1u8PQM0 **27** *Latino Daily News*, 11 Jan 2012, nin.tl/Y5WtUB **28** CBS news, 1 Dec 2011, nin.tl/1u8Rq0f **29** Fox news, 28 Sep 2007, nin.tl/Y5X34P **30** *SFGate*, 8 Dec 2011, nin.tl/1u8T4z9 **31** *Huffington Post*, 2 Jun 2012, nin.tl/Y5XNGX **32** *Guardian*, 9 Jan 2012, nin.tl/1u8UQjG **33** ACLU, nin.tl/Y5YpfE **34** *Guardian*, 4 Jun 2013, nin.tl/Y5Zmof **35** *Express*, 21 Apr 2013, nin.tl/1u8YYA0 **36** *The Lawyer*, 23 Sep 2013, nin.tl/Y60Qz3 **37** *Guardian*, 4 Jun 2013, nin.tl/1u94PFy **38** *Guardian*, 22 May 2013, nin.tl/1u95jLX **39** *Telegraph*, 29 May 2013, nin.tl/Y62mB5 **40** Law Careers.net, nin.tl/1u97zCN **41** *Guardian*, 27 Mar 2012, nin.tl/Y637tT

11
Civil liberties, human rights and democracy

'"Civil liberties" is another name for the political freedoms that we must have available to us all if it is to be true to say of us that we live in a society that adheres to the principle of representative, or democratic, government.'
Conor Gearty[1]

CIVIL liberties can loosely be described as encompassing: the right to vote, the right to life, freedom from torture, security of the person, the right to personal liberty and due process of law, freedom of expression and freedom of association. They are the legal underpinning of a democratic nation because, without them, the constituents of that democracy are not free to hold their government to account. If a populace is held in a state of fear and insecurity in their ability to cast their vote, express an opinion, withdraw their labour, or protest – they are unable to exercise their democratic mandate. They are unable to express free consent (or opposition) to the status quo.

Civil liberties, human rights and democracy itself are incompatible with the neoliberal political and economic paradigm. This is why the neoliberal project was first rolled out in dictatorships, such as Pinochet's Chile. This is why Structural Adjustment Programmes undermine labour laws, suppress wages and cut spending on education and public programmes – to de-civilize and disempower the population. The end game of Austerity is to de-civilize and disempower whole sections of the UK population, too. In order to do so, the legal underpinning of UK civilization is being unpicked.

The long road to civil liberties, human rights and democracy

The history books tell us that civil liberties in the UK were developed over three great charters.

The English Charter of Liberties

In the English Charter of Liberties of 1100, King Henry I extended rights to the nobility and church officials to secure his legitimacy as monarch.

The Magna Carta

Between 1213 and 1215 groups from across England came together to draft the Magna Carta. This 'Great Charter' was a schedule of protections against King John's arbitrary and exploitative use of feudal customs and abuse of the justice system. As Henry before him, John was forced to extend fuller protections and rights to maintain his position. Only 3 of the Magna Carta's 63 clauses remain in English law today, and one of them became the foundation for the modern justice system.

'No free man shall be seized or imprisoned, or stripped of his rights or possessions, or outlawed or exiled... nor will we proceed with force against him... except by the lawful judgment of his equals or by the law of the land. To no-one will we sell, to no-one deny or delay right or justice.' [2]

The Bill of Rights 1689

There was not another significant milestone in the development of civil liberties until the 17th century, with the Levellers. The Levellers were a group of civilian political activists during the English Civil War of 1642-1651. They are often credited as being the pioneers of democracy in the UK. This is a considerable exaggeration. They largely consisted of businesspeople and skilled craftspeople and, although they were England's first democratic political group, they did not advocate equal rights or democratic ideals for women, or for those outside their class. They campaigned for freedom of conscience on matters of religion, freedom from conscription into the armed forces, and that all laws 'apply equally to everyone: there must be no discrimination on grounds of tenure, estate, charter, degree, birth or place'.[3]

In 1647, things were beginning to reach critical mass. An over-taxed, over-conscripted population was getting sick of an unjust status quo. And, in October of that year, the New Model Army met *en masse* around Putney church to debate these ideas. The meetings were large, mutinous affairs, with regiments of the army debating ideas that would challenge the monarchy and ruling classes they existed to serve. They would be known in history as 'The Putney Debates'. Yet, at the time, there was a virtual news blackout. Newsbooks of the day reported that proceedings from Putney were 'not thought fit to be presented to the publique view'.[4] The Levellers, however, released their own record of the debates, in the shape of *An Agreement of the People*, a list of democratic demands made upon the ruling classes.[5] They had to wait four decades, but eventually their demands were answered, at least in part.

Following the Glorious Revolution of 1688, King James II fled England, the crown was given to William and Mary, but there was no legal monarch or parliament. A group of magistrates and ex-members of the House of Commons met on 22 January 1689 and passed an Act declaring themselves the true parliament of England. They in turn invited William and Mary to become monarchs under the Declaration of Right. They codified this arrangement with the Bill of Rights, which enshrined civil liberties in English law, and secured the authority of the parliamentary system.[6] The Bill of Rights included freedom to petition the monarch (a precursor to political protest rights); freedom from cruel and unusual punishment (this would lead to the ban on torture contained in our Human Rights Act); and freedom from being fined without trial. Powers over taxation and mobilizing the armed forces were passed from the monarchy to Parliament.

The 1832 Reform Act

But the kind of parliamentary democracy one might recognize today was still a very long way away. It wasn't until the 18th century that transcripts of parliamentary debates were made available for consumption by those outside. Prior to the 1774 Parliamentary Register, campaigned for by radical MP and journalist John Wilkes and others, the discussions of Westminster were held in complete secrecy.

As late as the 19th century, the entire voting population of England and Wales was just 366,000 people.[7] In fact, the parliamentary franchise had remained mostly unchanged between the Middle Ages and the Great Reform Act of 1832.[8] Qualifications to vote were different in each of the four nations making up the United Kingdom. But one thing was constant – women and the working classes had no part to play.

By the 19th century, the country was on the verge of revolution. The ruling Tory Party was steadfastly opposed to political reform and was ousted in 1830. Under the threat of political revolution, the Whig Party pushed through the Reform Act of 1832 which expanded the franchise to a total of 650,000 people (just 18 per cent of the total male population of England and Wales). Women and working-class men were still excluded from the democratic process, and votes were cast in public (secret ballots were not introduced until 1872).[9]

20th-century advances

It is clear that 'democratic' movements prior to the 20th century were mostly campaigns, first by the aristocracy and then by the industrial middle classes, to confer greater power, autonomy and privilege on themselves. The concessions from the ruling class of each day were largely made as power-sharing deals, rather than a transformation based on a notion of equality or any of the democratic ideals we might recognize today.

It wasn't until the 20th century that anything like proper democratic and human rights reached women and the working classes – when they were finally pushed beyond the bounds of tolerance.

First came the abomination of the First World War, in which 704,803 British soldiers lost their lives and almost 2.3 million were wounded. Then, in the year 1918/19, an estimated 40 million people worldwide died from the Spanish Flu – 250,000 of them in the UK, mostly between the ages of 15 and 35.[10]

In 1918, the Representation of the People Act greatly expanded suffrage within the UK. The vote was given to all men over the age of 21, with all property qualifications removed. Suffrage for propertied women over the age of 30 gave more than eight million women the opportunity to vote for the first time. The total franchise now stood at 21.4 million.[11]

But life for the working classes after World War One was still short and brutal. Almost immediately after the war, workers in most of Britain's key industries began to strike for higher wages, better working conditions and shorter hours. But socialism didn't take root, national industries were sold off and Liberal prime minister Lloyd George's coalition government believed that laissez-faire (capitalist) economics would bring the British economy back to life. It did not. During the 1920s the British economy failed to recover and unemployment hovered between 10 and 20 per cent. After the Wall Street Crash of 1929, things became markedly worse. That same year, Prime Minister Ramsay MacDonald created an all-party National Government to attempt to deal with the crisis. This government cut the wages of public-sector workers (teachers' pay fell by 15 per cent and that of the police by 12.5 per cent); it reduced National Insurance benefits and paid them for a shorter period of time; and it introduced a means test for the long-term unemployed on 'extended benefits'.[12] It sounds remarkably familiar to the economic tactics of today. So did it work?

By 1932, unemployment had risen to 22.5 per cent – at a time when most households still had only one breadwinner due to restrictions on female labour.[13] Workers faced either exploitative and dangerous working conditions to earn poverty wages or else complete destitution. Unemployment did not dip below one million until 1940 during World War Two. The period was marked by mass strikes, including the General Strike of 1926, which saw over 1.7 million working people strike for nine days to prevent efforts to decrease their pay while increasing their working hours.[14] In 1932, 2,500 starving unemployed people took part in the Jarrow March to highlight the poverty-induced hunger of working-class Britons.

After the Second World War, the British working classes made it clear they were not willing to accept the horrors of the inter-war period all over again. They voted out Conservative wartime prime minister Winston Churchill, and elected Clement Attlee's Labour Party, which ran on a socialist platform of nationalization and collectivism. At this point, the conversation on human rights took a further step – it went beyond a mere vote. People understood, from the horrendous experiences of the previous century, that capitalism did not necessarily equate to social progress. They realized that in order for the broadest number to share the benefits of wealth creation, human rights needed to be extended – to protect working people from exploitation, to protect the inevitable unemployed people from poverty and destitution, to create equal access to quality education and healthcare, to create decent homes that people could afford to live in. They saw that all of these rights were necessary to create a social progress consummate with any economic progress. The modern welfare state was born, and with it a flurry of civil liberties were gained throughout the latter half of the 20th century.

Finally, in 1998, the New Labour government signed the European Convention on Human Rights into British law, providing a legal underpinning to this enshrinement of our civil liberties.

The road to civil liberties in Britain winds through almost a thousand years. Each of these advances was granted under duress by unwilling figures of authority. But in reality, the kind of civil liberties, human rights and democracy many of us recognize or believe we benefit from today, only came into being within living memory. Such rights were only established through the courage and enormous sacrifice of the trade union movement, the suffragettes, the Jarrow Marchers, the General Strikers, the post-War Labour Party and the millions of people who refused to tolerate the absence of a just system. They were not gifted, they did not naturally evolve; they were fought for and won.

They were so well won that despite being but half a century old, they are taken for granted by many today – and, regrettably, not appreciated. A bizarre idea has been propagated that capitalism brought us these rights, when they were actually won from capitalists. They exist to protect individuals from both state and corporate exploitation. They exist outside of any economic model.

Nevertheless, many people are unaware of or unalarmed by the current rapid erosion of these rights and liberties.

Personal liberty and due process before the law

Since the passing of the Habeas Corpus Act in 1649, citizens have been protected from false and arbitrary imprisonment by being presumed innocent until proof of their guilt is established by a jury of their peers in an independent court. Yet successive governments have passed legislation that seriously undermines this principle, and allows the state and its police force to restrict liberty and confine citizens without interference by the courts.

Detention without charge

Prior to 1984, a person could not be held by police for longer than 24 hours without a criminal charge being made against them. The Thatcher government extended this to four days; New Labour extended this first to 7 days, then to 14 days, and finally sought the power to detain citizens without charge for up to 90 days, at the request of the police.

Whilst the Blair government was defeated on 90-day detention without charge, the period was nevertheless doubled to 28 days.

The Coalition allowed this legislation to expire in 2011, returning the period to 14 days, only to apply for permission to extend to 28 days in the same year.[15] Meanwhile, the Anti-Terrorism and Security Act 2001 allowed for indefinite detention of non-British citizens suspected of committing terrorist acts, where there was not enough evidence to proceed to a court of law.

Unlawful imprisonment

The Control Orders legislation passed in the 2006 Terrorism Act meant that anybody suspected of terrorist-related activities by the Home Secretary (but not convicted by a court), could be electronically tagged, monitored, restricted from making phone calls or using the internet, banned from certain kinds of work, have their movement restricted, their passport revoked and be obliged to report to the police.

In response to criticism of such powers, the Coalition government did not extend the life of Control Orders, but replaced them with Terrorism Prevention and Investigation Measures (TPIMS). This saw two improvements: a two-year time limit on the orders, and the required judicial approval of measures.

However, the government later created legislation for Enhanced TPIMS, bringing back many of the powers of the Control Orders. This includes a complete ban on the use of electronic communications, and being ordered to relocate to any address that the Home Secretary chooses.

Secret courts

The 700-year-old tradition of open justice has been under attack from successive pieces of legislation since 1997 that have allowed 'closed material proceedings' or secret courts into the justice system. First introduced in 1997 for immigration trials, they were later used for Control Order and TPIM-related charges.[16] Yet, in a stunning move in March 2013, the Coalition government and parliament approved legislation to introduce secret courts into civil cases. If a citizen takes the British government or its officials to court in cases of torture, rendition, or a whole host of other eventualities, the government is able to present evidence to the judge to which the claimant, defendant, media and public will never be privy. This will allow the government to resist due scrutiny for its role in torture, rendition and other crimes. The Reverend Nicholas Mercer, a lieutenant colonel who was the army's most senior lawyer during the last Iraq war, told the *Daily Mail*:

'The justice and security bill has one principal aim and that is to cover up UK complicity in rendition and torture. The bill is an affront to the open justice on which this country rightly prides itself and, above all, it is an affront to human dignity.'[17]

Freedom of expression and assembly

Perhaps the most readily noticeable restrictions on liberty have been in the arena of freedom of expression and assembly. The rise in so-called 'anti-terror' legislation, especially since 2001, has had a massive impact on people's ability to organize sizable demonstrations, marches and actions without the threat of increasing militarized police force.

The Thatcher government's Public Order Act of 1986 sought to prevent the effectiveness of public protest by requiring organizers to give police six days' advance notice of their action. Since this time, successive governments have used upgrades to the Public Order Act to undermine the right to peaceful protest.

The Serious and Organized Crime and Police Act 2005 granted a number of powers to police and restricted protesters in a number of different ways. In response to the single-handed protest of Brian Haw, who occupied Parliament Square for several years in opposition to the crimes of the Iraq War, the Act applied special restrictions on protest within a designated area of one kilometre from Parliament Square. As a result it is now virtually impossible to protest outside the UK parliament without being arrested.

The Act created a new offence of trespassing on a designated site, such as Crown land or land considered by a Secretary of State to be off limits in the interests of national security.

The Act also made **all** these newly created offences arrestable, whereas previously a police officer had to determine whether they suspected a person of committing a non-arrestable, arrestable or serious arrestable offence.

In addition to these new legal restrictions, there has been a gradual militarization of the police force, which has been armed with an ever-growing toolkit of measures and devices to quell dissent in the streets. These include:

Kettling – This is where police officers, vans and cars are used to create a pop-up prison around groups of protesters, keeping them confined to a space and stipulating conditions such as providing identification or being photographed, in order to leave without arrest.

Snatch and grab arrests – Here, groups of police form a moving corridor into the protest, the front officers of which grab protesters at random. These arrests can also be made by lines outside a kettle, or by plain-clothes police in advance of protests.[18]

Agents provocateurs and violence – This was witnessed at the 2010 student protests where *agents provocateurs* were filmed running into the crowds, pushing, pulling and kicking student protesters in order to generate violent conditions.[19] One student named Alfie Meadows ended up in hospital requiring brain surgery after a police officer beat him with a baton. Instead of the police officer facing the courts, Alfie was charged with violent disorder. He was finally acquitted in March 2013, by a jury who agreed he was defending himself and other protesters.

Martial law and emergency powers

Since the Bill of Rights Act 1689, it has been illegal for the

British government to dispatch the armed forces to British streets during peace time without the consent of parliament. For hundreds of years we have lived under an agreement that dissenting citizens faced police rather than the armed forces. The Civil Contingencies Act 2004 ended this tradition. The Act means that a range of emergency powers can be applied by approval of the monarch (the government) which would suspend the Bill of Rights 1689, Habeas Corpus and others for a period of up to 21 days at a time.

The surveillance state

The exponential rise in surveillance permitted by law in the UK is astounding. Until 1986 there were severe restrictions on the ability of police and state to surveil UK citizens; phone tapping and the interception of private communications were inadmissible in courts and heavily penalized. However, since 1986, an altogether different approach has been adopted.

The Thatcher government's Interception of Communications Act 1985 gave permission for phone tapping. However, the New Labour era saw a massive roll-out in surveillance in the name of the 'war on terror'.

The Regulation of Investigatory Powers Act 2000 allowed the government full surveillance powers over all kinds of communications. The Act's main provisions allow five new categories of surveillance, from bugging of phones to spying on and intercepting communications. It allows the Home Secretary to issue an interception warrant to examine the contents of letters or communications on various grounds, including *in the interests of the economic wellbeing of the United Kingdom*. It also prevents the existence of interception warrants, and any and all data collected with them, from being revealed in court.

It enables the police, intelligence services, HM Revenue and Customs (and several hundred more public bodies, including local authorities and a wide range of regulators) to demand telephone, internet and postal-service providers to hand over detailed communications records for individual users. This can include name and address, phone calls made and received, source and destination of emails, internet browsing information and mobile-phone data that records the user's location. These powers are self-authorized by the body concerned, with no external or judicial oversight.

These powers have been extensively overused by police, councils and other enforcement agencies. The Act has rightly been deemed a 'snooper's charter'. Warrants are currently being issued at a rate of around 30 a week. In the 15 months from July 2005 to October 2006, 2,407 warrants were issued.[20] One of the more egregious misuses of the power occurred in 2008, when Poole Borough Council put three children and their parents under surveillance to check they were in the catchment area for the school they had applied to.[21] The council had directly surveilled the family 21 times. Other councils have launched undercover operations on dog fouling and fly tipping. In 2011, HMRC tax solicitor Osita Mba used whistleblowing procedures to bring attention to secret sweetheart deals between Dave Hartnett, the Chief of the HMRC, and tax-evading corporations. These shady deals were made without legal advice and cost the UK millions in lost taxes. In 2013, it was revealed that the HMRC used its powers under the Act to harass and surveil Mr Mba and his wife (their personal mobile phone records, tax affairs, internet histories and email accounts were interrogated), in efforts to intimidate him or find incriminating evidence with which to quash his whistleblowing.[22]

There has also been a rise in CCTV operations: the filming of people in public spaces. Britain has gone from zero to over four million CCTV cameras in recent decades, and now has a higher number of cameras than China despite being a small fraction of the size.[23] Cameras are also increasingly hidden and disguised as light fittings, plant pots and other innocuous items in our urban landscape. Surely, if the aim were to prevent crime, the cameras would be clearly visible? Despite all this surveillance, there is less than one arrest per day that results from CCTV footage.[24]

Formalizing Britain's police state

In March 2014 new government legislation made any behaviour perceived to potentially 'cause nuisance or annoyance' a criminal offence. The Anti-Social Behaviour, Crime and Policing Bill also grants local authorities, police and even private security firms sweeping powers to bar citizens from assembling lawfully in public spaces. Those who refuse orders under the new rules will face arrest, fines and even prison time.

Since the Crime and Disorder Act 1998, which introduced Anti-Social Behaviour Orders (ASBOs), the government has invented and legislated for a litany of such orders covering everything from dog poo to drug addiction, including but not limited to: Control Orders; Terrorism Prevention and Investigation Measures Orders; Intervention Orders; Crack House Closure Orders; Premise Closure Orders; Brothel Closure Orders; Gang Related Violence Injunctions; Designated Public Place Orders; Special Interim Management Orders; Gating Orders; Dog Control Orders; Letter Clearing Notices; Noise Abatement Orders; Graffiti/Defacement Removal Notices; Directions to Leave and Dispersal Orders.

The Anti-Social Behaviour, Crime and Policing Bill purports to simplify this legacy of New Labour legislative promiscuity. In reality, it creates a series of wildly ambiguous, generic orders that grant officers of the state and private sector even greater powers to issue tougher sentences, with fewer checks and balances to protect citizens.[25]

Injunctions to Prevent Nuisance and Annoyance (IPNAs)

The Bill introduces Injunctions to Prevent Nuisance and Annoyance (IPNAs) to replace ASBOs. Almost no-one will be sad to say goodbye to ASBOs. The orders, designed to allow police to tackle anti-social behaviour, simply became a means of criminalizing youthful indiscretion – and eventually a means of criminalizing anything people found annoying. Some of the bizarre abuses of this power include:

- Stuart Hunt of Loch Ness has been brought to court 100 times since 2007 for breaching an ASBO preventing him from laughing, staring or slow hand-clapping.[26]
- Homeless, alcoholic and mentally ill Michael Gilligan was given a 99-year ASBO rather than the welfare support that might have made a difference.[27]
- A profoundly deaf 17-year-old girl was given an ASBO and a jail sentence for spitting in the street.[28]
- A 13-year-old was banned from using the word 'grass' in England or Wales.
- Manchester Council applied an ASBO to prevent a mobile soup kitchen from feeding the homeless.
- Councils have placed ASBOs on homeless people, resulting in prison sentences for begging 'earnestly and humbly'.
- An 87-year-old man was given an ASBO threatening a prison sentence if he was sarcastic to his neighbours.[29]

The ASBO has allowed the line between criminal behaviour and annoying behaviour to become hopelessly blurred – and the IPNAs will only serve to exacerbate the problem. We have seen the abuses permitted under ASBO legislation, the test for which included wording to the effect that ASBOs could only be issued where an actual act of 'harassment, alarm or distress' had occurred. IPNAs have a much weaker test, applicable where on the 'balance of probabilities' a person has *or might* engage in behaviour 'capable of causing annoyance' to another person.[30] How many times a day could this legislation apply to any of us? Eating with our mouths open, talking too loudly into our phones in a public space, walking too slowly or quickly or belching without saying 'pardon me'. All of this may very well cause annoyance – but soon it might well also be illegal.

An IPNA can be applied for by local authorities, police, some transport bodies and some NHS authorities. The orders can be issued to anyone aged 10 or over, and there is no limit on how long an IPNA can be applied to a person aged 18 and over. A person could receive an IPNA aged 18 and retain it their entire life.

Whereas an ASBO could only require the subject to desist from certain actions, the IPNA includes 'positive obligations'. This means the subject of an IPNA can be found in breach not simply for *doing* things they have been banned from doing, but from *not doing* things that the IPNA states they must. This makes an IPNA much closer to probation and other post-conviction arrangements than to a civil order.

The consequences of breaching an IPNA are serious. The breaching of an IPNA has been added to the conditions for securing possession of a home – meaning that a 10-year-old child breaching their IPNA could result in their entire family being evicted from their council house. Breaching the orders can also result in jail time for anyone over 14.[31]

Even the Association of Chief Police Officers (ACPO), giving evidence on the original proposals, argued that this could lead to further criminalization of children and called on the government to think again. In a letter to the *Observer* newspaper, Children's Commissioner Dr Maggie Atkinson and a host of children's charities wrote 'We acknowledge that antisocial behaviour can blight the lives of individuals and communities, but this bill is not the answer. It promotes intolerance of youth, is a blow for civil liberties and will damage children's relationship with the police. Children learn the importance of right and wrong from their parents, teachers and communities. We do not need to create more laws to do it.'[32]

But the plans move along unaltered.

Public Spaces Protection Orders

Public Spaces Protection Orders (PSPOs) and new Dispersal Orders will replace Designated Public Space Orders, Dog Control Orders, Gating Orders and a host of other orders intended to keep aggressive drunken people, or drug dealers or dog poo off our streets. But it is plain that the target for these laws is no longer the person peddling illegal drugs, but the people sharing politically challenging ideas.

These new powers present the most significant threat to lawful assembly and protest in modern history.

PSPOs will be granted where 'activities carried on *or likely* to be carried on in a public place will have or have had a detrimental effect on the quality of life of those in the locality'.[33] They can be used to restrict an activity or to require people to perform an activity in a certain way.[34] They require substantially less consultation than current alcohol-free zones or dog-control zones and, rather than applying to everyone, they can be applied to specific groups of people (the homeless, the unemployed, racial/religious groups etc) – opening the door to discrimination. These rules could see homeless people or young people lawfully excluded from public spaces.

PSPOs are subject to 'on the spot' fines, rather than attendance at a magistrates' court, reducing the scrutiny and checks on police power. They are also by no means short term. They can be applied for up to three years, and continued for another three years at the end of their term.

The Orders have been strongly challenged by UK human rights organization Liberty and freedom campaigners The Manifesto Club on the basis that they will seriously infringe upon people's freedom to assemble, associate and protest. The Ramblers (the walking charity) have also given written evidence to the government, voicing their fears about the further appropriation of public highways, byways and footpaths under PSPO powers.

Dispersal Orders

Under the current Direction to Leave powers, anyone over 10 years of age can be asked to disperse from a 'locality' and stay dispersed for a period not exceeding 48 hours. The previous Dispersal Orders meant that a Police Superintendent (or an officer with specific written authority from the Superintendent) could disperse groups of two or more people in areas where there had been 'persistent anti-social behaviour' or take home any young person under the age of 16 who was in a dispersal zone between 9pm and 6am. Anyone failing to comply with a Dispersal Order faced a fine of up to £2,500 or up to three months in prison.[35]

Downing Street clearly did not feel this was tough enough. The enhanced Dispersal Powers within the new Bill enable police constables and even Police Community Support Officers (PCSOs) to issue dispersal orders if they *think* a group of two or more persons *might* harass, alarm or distress others in the vicinity. The PCSO or constable can specify how long the person or group must remain out of the designated area, by which route they must leave, and confiscate any items of their property that they deem 'anti-social'. Failure to comply with any element of these orders results in a fine of up to £5,000 or three months in prison. The new legislation also fails to define 'locality' – meaning a person could in theory be excluded from a city, a county or even a whole country.[36]

These new laws effectively end freedom of assembly in England and Wales, as any lawful assembly can be instantly redefined as illegal on the spot by a part-time PCSO, people's personal possessions can be confiscated, and anyone who dares to challenge the process may end up in jail.

Many believe they have rights to protest, assemble and associate that they actually lost a decade ago, simply because they have never actually attempted to claim these rights. They remain imaginary freedoms, never cashed in.

The war on internet freedom

In a time when unionizing, protesting, political meetings, withdrawal of labour through strike and other historic sources of dissent have been outlawed, criminalized or stigmatized, internet freedom has become a proxy for actual freedom.

While providing an important space and network to disseminate information and apply pressure, the internet needs to be viewed as an additional tool with which to share ideas, and not a replacement for actual demonstration. A twitter storm is never going to have the impact of a general strike. Yet even this last haven for resistance is under threat as corporatized governments seek to lock down dissent.

In June 2013, the *Guardian* newspaper released the first of a mass of documentation from National Security Agency (NSA) whistleblower Edward Snowden that confirms the existence of a massive US surveillance programme on ordinary civilians across the globe.[37] These documents revealed that governments and military intelligence are indeed given privy access to the internet, email and social media accounts of civilians across the world, without warrant, and without their knowledge. This is not in dispute.

The key findings from the documents leaked by Snowden have been explosive.

PRISM

PRISM is a $20-million-a-year surveillance programme run by the NSA, the intelligence wing of the US military. It allows direct access to the data of internet giants Facebook, Google, Apple, Microsoft and Skype – to name but a few. It allows US spies to access historical data (email, video, file transfers, images and private chats/messages) and live monitor Skype calls and other communications. In short, they can access anyone's entire communications history, and listen to or watch individuals communicating in real time – all without any judicial intervention. The documents also state that the internet companies are complicit in PRISM.

The programme has been running since 2007, and throughout this time, representatives of the State and of the internet companies involved have dismissed allegations that such a programme existed, or could ever exist. We now know they lied.

According to *The Guardian*: 'When the NSA reviews a communication it believes merits further investigation, it issues what it calls a "report". According to the NSA, "over 2,000 PRISM-based reports" are now issued every month. There were 24,005 in 2012, a 27-per-cent increase on the previous year. In total, more than 77,000 intelligence reports have cited the PRISM program.' [38]

The UK public reacted by wanting to know what role the UK government, armed forces and security agencies had played in PRISM. Was there a UK version of PRISM that they were unaware of? Foreign Secretary William Hague described these claims as 'fanciful nonsense', insisting UK citizens had 'nothing to fear' from PRISM.[39]

Despite these assurances, the next release of Snowden's files exposed the UK's own internet surveillance operation: Project Tempora.

Project Tempora

Government Communications Headquarters (GCHQ) is the secretive cyber-security agency for 'the Government, the Armed Services, Law Enforcement and industry'.[40] Since 2007, GCHQ has been running a programme called 'Mastering the Internet'. Its aim is to create a way of accessing, analysing and utilizing online activity and communications. In order to do this, Project Tempora sought to create an 'internet buffer' – a means of collecting and storing masses of online activity to review and analyse later, through the Cheltenham Processing Centre. The data is stored for 30 days while GCHQ staff browse through it, collecting intelligence.

In a 2010/11 midyear review, the Mastering the Internet programme announced a stunning achievement, that it had 'delivered the next big step in the access, processing and storage journey, hitting a new high of more than 39 billion events in a 24-hour period, dramatically increasing our capability to produce unique intelligence from our targets' use of the internet and made [sic] major contributions to recent operations.'

By February 2011, the team was proudly declaring that the Cheltenham Processing Centre now 'produces larger amounts of metadata collection than the NSA'.[41]

This 'deep dive capability' was made possible by GCHQ literally plugging in to the fibre-optic network that acts as the spine of the internet – and pulling out any internet traffic entering or leaving the UK in real time. Anyone who sends an email, makes a phone call over the internet, or sends a message using social media platforms can no longer do so in the belief that this communication is private.

This makes Tempora a significantly more invasive and larger-scale surveillance programme than PRISM. While most other government departments have been suffering budget cuts, the Treasury found an extra £650 million to spend on 'cyber security', with more than half of these funds going to GCHQ and its Mastering the Internet programme.

Phone data collection

In a project started under the administration of George W Bush, the NSA has been collecting the phone-call data of millions of Americans. The NSA issued a secret court order to phone company Verizon, requiring it to submit reports on 'an ongoing daily basis'. Each day, Verizon provides the NSA with the full data of who called who, when and for how long. The contents of the calls are not recorded, but it gives the NSA unprecedented oversight of the relationships of private citizens.[42]

Busting encryption

The NSA and GCHQ have been collaborating to undermine online encryption programmes used by public, foreign governments and companies to secure the privacy of their internet communications. They have broadly compromised the guarantees that internet companies have given consumers to reassure them that their communications, online banking and medical records are indecipherable to criminals or governments.

The agencies have adopted a battery of methods in their systematic and ongoing assault on what they see as one of the biggest threats to their ability to access huge swathes of internet traffic –'the use of ubiquitous encryption across the internet'.[43] The agencies worked covertly with technology companies to slip weaknesses into encryption and security programmes. The agencies then exploit these known vulnerabilities to unlock passwords and encryption to email accounts, bank accounts, medical records and other information mistakenly thought to be protected. Technology companies and Internet Service Providers have been compensated by the US and UK governments to provide a back door through the security software they sell their customers.

This is not the end of the story, but the initial unravelling of a conspiracy of lies about the true nature of the surveillance state. Yet, if it were not for the admirable efforts of Edward Snowden, journalist Glenn Greenwald, and the courage of the *Guardian* editorial team, we would still believe PRISM was 'fanciful nonsense'.

But it is not only a misplaced fear of 'terror' that has been used to ramp up the war on the internet.

The phoney war on porn

David Cameron has announced a 'war on porn' – asking Internet Service Providers (ISPs) to filter people's internet usage automatically, with anything classed as 'porn' inaccessible without the user specifically requesting access to it. Not only is this idea unworkable, but it is entirely cynical. David Cameron is attempting a bloodless coup of the free internet, inside a *papier mâché* Trojan Horse of *Daily Mail* headlines.

The plan began with Claire Perry MP, Cameron's special advisor on 'preventing the commercialization and sexualization of childhood'. Perry launched a moral crusade in response to a campaign by the *Daily Mail*, which (on news of Cameron's plans) announced victory in its war on porn.[44] On the same page the *Mail* featured pictures of 17-year-old model Kendall Jenner urging readers to check out her 'model figure in an aqua bikini'.[45] Readers were also treated to the cleavage of Kourtney Kardashian alongside the headline 'No Sudden Movements! Kourtney Kardashian shows her body confidence in daring low cut Swimsuit – she knows how to show off her assets'.[46] Cute.

Nevertheless, the government seized on the *Mail* campaign and began to pressure Internet Service Providers to operate a 'default on' porn filter. In future, anyone setting up their broadband connection will have to actively request access to porn, as the filter will be the default.

Until these new rules, the Obscene Publications Act has governed what it is legal and illegal to publish in England and Wales. Henceforth, the government has declared that those images which are not currently illegal, yet are considered beyond the pale by the moral majority, become prosecutable.

Speaking to the BBC, one source at an ISP gave his reasons why this policy is most likely unworkable:

'It sounds like a good idea until you think it through... There are three reasons why it doesn't work. First it may be illegal under the Regulation of Investigatory Powers. Then there's the fact that no filter is perfect, and finally kids are smart enough to find their way around them.'[47]

A source at another company saw another reason why 'default on' (sites labelled as 'porn' being blocked by default) might be a bad idea: 'It makes parents complacent – if you tell them the filter is switched on by default, they get a false sense of security. We want parents to make informed choices about the way their children use the internet.'[48]

These reasons focus around workability. But there are other reasons besides this that need to be addressed.

First, there is the case against the nanny state. The government has cut the budget for Legal Aid, is forcing disabled, sick and mentally ill people off their social security and is selling off schools and hospitals to private interests at a gallop. If the government argues that the state has no role in these core elements of our society – why on earth would they think the state has a role in telling people whether they can watch porn or not, or in deciding what is and is not porn? It just doesn't make sense.

Second, privacy and freedom. How will data on who requests porn or not be stored and used? Does anyone requesting removal of the porn filter become somehow suspect? Will it become lawful for someone to have their internet usage monitored where they have requested the filter removed, the act itself becoming a red flag?

Worse than all this, the move sets a precedent. The state is now telling people what they can and cannot view on the internet – beyond the confines of the law. It might well be legal, but it is not state sanctioned. It will mean a permissive relationship between government and ISP – government asks, ISP does. It also leads to some technical infrastructure changes that will mean internet usage can be more easily controlled and monitored in future.

The government's claim to be acting in the interests of protecting children also contradicts its behaviour in other areas. The coalition government cut the budget for CEOP, the government's online child safety watchdog, by fully 10 per cent in 2012.[49] All the indications are that this policy is about talking tough for the sake of appeasing sections of the press and the electorate, while gaining greater control over the internet. Opponents of the scheme also find themselves in a morally unsteady footing – who can argue against ending child-abuse photos online?

Just a few short years ago, repressive countries' restriction of the internet access of their citizens met with the scorn of the 'civilized West'. Those days are gone. The revelations of NSA whistleblower Edward Snowden show just how closely and arbitrarily internet communications are being monitored in the UK, Europe and the US – and how feeble our protections from such abuses of power truly are.

Given that employers are already hiring and firing based

on a person's social-media activity – with some even making employment contingent upon surrendering passwords to personal social media accounts for monitoring – one suspects this is little more than the thin end of the wedge.[50]

With the Conservative Party promising to abolish the Human Rights Act if it wins the next election, we are facing the complete revocation of the legal underpinning of our civil liberties.[51]

All of these regressive changes are founded on the fixed neoliberal belief that what is best for 'business' is best for all of us. Yet it is demonstrably true that, in many areas of economic policy, what is best for business comes at the expense of the public interest. If the profits of business are not being shared with those responsible for delivering them, what is the point? Today, profits are rising as a direct result of the exploitation of the majority of people, who are working day in and day out to deliver them.

As more people become aware of the exploitative nature of the system and institutions governing their lives, democracy becomes an ever greater threat to the neoliberal project. This is why civil liberties, human rights and the other fundamental tenets of democracy are being curtailed so expeditiously. The endgame will be the creation of globalized legal frameworks making Austerity permanent, and enforceable through international law.

1 Conor Gearty, *Civil Liberties*, Oxford University Press, 2007. **2** British Library, nin.tl/1oYvDD2 **3** Liberty, nin.tl/1oYxjwy **4** Michael Mendle, *The Putney Debates of 1647: The Army, the Levellers and the English State*, Cambridge University Press, 2001. **5** constitution.org, nin.tl/1INmaU1 **6** John Patterson, *The Bill of Rights: Politics, Religion, and the Quest for Justice*, Universe, 2004, p 40. **7** Liberty, op cit. **8** Neil Johnston, 'The History of the Parliamentary Franchise', Mar 2013, nin.tl/ZC8XTY **9** Ibid. **10** virus.stanford.edu/uda **11** parliament.uk, nin.tl/1INoWZx **12** Rosemary Rees, *Poverty and Public Health 1815-1948*, Heinemann, 2001. **13** J Volenec, *The Influence of Class on Social Life in Britain Between the Wars*, University of Pardubice, 2006. **14** BBC news, nin.tl/WyTTVx **15** *The Guardian*, 23 Jun 2011, nin.tl/1INsF9p **16** Liberty, nin.tl/1INtj6X **17** *Daily Mail*, 27 Feb 2013, nin.tl/WyYlmV **18** See video examples at nin.tl/1INv5ow & nin.tl/Wz08bR **19** See a video example at nin.tl/1INvIDW **20** Wikipedia, nin.tl/Wz2w2k **21** BBC news, 10 Apr 2008, nin.tl/1INwATL **22** Richard Murphy, *Guardian* comment is free, nin.tl/Wz3KdR **23** *Daily Mail*, 11 Aug 2009, nin.tl/Wz4Ar5 **24** Ibid. **25** Liberty briefing, Feb 2013, nin.tl/WTkUDt **26** *Daily Mail*, 19 Jul 2013, nin.tl/1qF7IhB **27** *Herald Scotland*, 10 Dec 2008, nin.tl/WTmWUc **28** Children & Young People Now, nin.tl/1qCsidz **29** Last four examples all from Parliament.uk, nin.tl/1ry5alJ **30** Steeles Law solicitors, nin.tl/1qCtqOk **31** *Telegraph*, 29 Jan 2013, nin.tl WToYDO **32** *Observer*, 13 Oct 2013, nin.tl/1qFaxPN **33** Liberty briefing, Feb 2013, nin.tl/WTkUDt **34** Manifesto Club, May 2013, nin.tl/1qFbS9e **35** CPS.gov.uk, nin.tl/WTsqOG **36** Liberty briefing, Feb 2013, nin.tl/WTkUDt **37** *Independent*, 10 Sep 2014, nin.tl/1qFeBiP **38** *Guardian*, 7 Jun 2013, nin.tl/WTwzSD **39** *Independent*, 10 Jun 2013, nin.tl/1qFfKa4 **40** GCHQ, nin.tl/WTyM0z **41** *Guardian*, 21 Jun 2013, nin tl/1qFhdND **42** *Guardian*, 6 Jun 2013, nin.tl/WTBByv **43** *Guardian*, 6 Sep 2013, nin.tl/1qFoeOG **44** *Daily Mail*, 22 Jul 2013, nin.tl/1qFiPXL **45** *Daily Mail*, 22 Jul 2013, nin.tl/WTHXOv **46** *Daily Mail*, 22 Jul 2013, nin.tl/WTLWdX **47** BBC news, 15 Jul 2013, nin.tl/WTNMvq **48** Ibid. **49** BBC news, 7 Feb 2012, nin.tl/1qFqB3Y **50** HR Examiner, 25 Feb 2013, nin.tl/WTPzk7 **51** BBC news, 9 Mar 2013, nin.tl/1qFrk5e

12
The endgame of Austerity

THE Trans Pacific Partnership (TPP) and the Transatlantic Trade and Investment Partnership (TTIP) are the largest trade agreements in history, and yet are not open for review, debate or amendment by national parliaments or the public. They seek to enshrine the rights of corporations under international law, restricting future governments from overturning Austerity policies, through fear of costly legal action or military intervention.

The Trans Pacific Partnership (TPP)

The TPP is an agreement between the US and 11 other Pacific Rim countries representing 40 per cent of global GDP, and has been under negotiation for three years.[1] The US, Canada, Australia, New Zealand, Japan, Mexico, Malaysia, Chile, Singapore, Peru, Vietnam, and Brunei will shortly be signing up to the TPP, with only a handful of people in each nation aware of the content of the deal.

Only three individuals in each TPP nation have been given full access to the agreement, while 600 'trade advisors' – lobbyists from corporations such as Monsanto, Chevron, Halliburton and Walmart – have been granted access.[2]

In fact, if it were not for WikiLeaks, the public (and the majority of their elected representatives) would still be unaware of the contents of the TPP. In mid-November 2013, WikiLeaks published a draft chapter of the agreement – and the reasons for secrecy became clear. This agreement tips the balance of corporate and democratic power firmly in favour of corporations.

Wikileaks chose to publish the draft TPP chapter on intellectual property (IP) 'due to its wide-ranging effects on medicines, publishers, internet services, civil liberties and biological patents'. The subsections of the chapter make 'agreements relating to patents (who may produce goods or drugs), copyright (who may transmit information), trademarks (who may describe information or goods as authentic) and industrial design.'

And as WikiLeaks states in its press release:

'The longest section of the chapter – 'Enforcement' – is devoted to detailing new policing measures, with far-reaching implications for individual rights, civil liberties, publishers, internet service providers and internet privacy, as well as for the creative, intellectual, biological and environmental commons. Particular measures proposed include supranational litigation tribunals to which sovereign national courts are expected to defer, but which have no human rights safeguards. The TPP IP chapter states that these courts can conduct hearings with secret evidence. The IP chapter also replicates many of the surveillance and enforcement provisions from the shelved SOPA and ACTA treaties.'

All this was contained in 30,000 words; just one chapter of this agreement.

TPP is the forerunner for its sister project – the EU/US Transatlantic Trade and Investment Partnership (TTIP). This next agreement rolls out the principles of the TPP across the EU and the UK.

The Transatlantic Trade and Investment Partnership (TTIP)

The TTIP is a secret agreement, negotiated behind closed doors by anonymous technocrats. This agreement will deliver the corporate privilege of TPP to the EU and UK, with the same lack of democratic scrutiny.

In early 2013, the EU announced that a High Level Working Group on Jobs and Growth, led by US Trade Representative Ron Kirk and EU Trade Commissioner Karel De Gucht, would research and report on plans to proceed with negotiations for the TTIP. Then it started to get weird. The EU did not produce a list of the membership of this group. Furthermore, all subsequent reports failed to mention authorship, contributors, or even the names of those reviewing or approving the reports for release.

Research and campaign organization Corporate Europe Observatory issued a freedom of information request to garner this information and were told 'there is no document containing the list of authors of the reports', and therefore that the matter did not fall under freedom of information rules.[3]

A quick look at the website of the working group shows that 65 per cent of the input for the two public consultations on the EU/US trade agreement came from companies and industry associations. Corporate Europe Observatory rightly asks: 'But who were the 114 respondents? What are they lobbying for?'

The answer is: we don't know, and those who do are refusing to tell us. What we do know, is the scope of the agreement. The final report of the anonymous High Level Working Group and a briefing paper from the UK government tell us that the final agreement will seek to achieve the same ends as TPP.[4] Key areas for concern are:

Trade tariffs – These remove ability of states to protect their domestic markets by placing tariffs on imported goods and services to make them less competitive.

Intellectual property – Further to the revelation of the TPP chapter on intellectual property released by WikiLeaks, internet censorship may also be the endgame here. The US-led Anti-Counterfeiting Trade Agreement (ACTA) claimed to target copyright infringement, but was identified as a potential means of policing the internet, with high financial penalties and prison time for file sharing. At first, 22 EU member states signed up to ACTA, but internet freedom campaigners elevated the argument and succeeded in mobilizing significant public opposition across the EU. The European Parliament struck down ACTA in July 2012, protecting member states from the legislation.[5] Despite protestations to the contrary, the TTIP could bring in ACTA through the back door, in secret, without the requirement for a democratic mandate.

Investor-state disputes – These are already in use across the world, allowing corporations to sue any nation daring to implement legislation protecting people and planet – investor-state disputes will be significantly expanded under TTIP. Given that US firm Walmart has a larger GDP than 157 countries in the world, including Norway, South Africa and Luxembourg – many states would be financially outgunned by corporations seeking to over-rule them.[6]

Food standards – The EU has stricter rules than the US on food production, particularly around Genetically Modified (GM) foods and meat. For instance, chlorine-washed chicken and the use of growth hormones in the production of livestock are banned in the EU, but are permitted in the US. US President Barack Obama has explicitly stated plans to use TTIP to overturn these (as he sees them) 'unscientific rules'.[7]

Corporate power vs state power

Proponents of capitalism who so vociferously oppose the threat of state power (even in a democratic state) appear to have no such issues with the rise of corporate power, which has no democratic foundation or restraint whatsoever. This is either gross naivety, or complicity in what is, ostensibly, a corporate coup.

A significant number of corporations now have greater financial power than the majority of states, and they have used this to infiltrate and leverage the structural power of states to implement laws and subsidies on their behalf. These trade agreements remove the protections of the EU, the US and the Pacific Rim countries (many of the world's most developed democracies) that have allowed for a social progress unthinkable in nations without them. Ultimately, this will lead to the de-civilization of the developed democracies. We know this from examining the fates of those countries already shackled to such trade agreements and rules.

Removal of tariffs

In a perfect world, protectionism through taxing imports would be unnecessary and rightly condemned. But we don't live in a perfect free market on a level playing field. Instead, we have a small number of overwhelmingly powerful corporations and national economies using the theory of 'trade liberalization' to decimate the internal markets of smaller nations to their own advantage.

One such example is rice and Haiti. Thirty years ago, Haiti could feed itself. A rapidly growing and developing population meant that, by the late 1980s, it had begun to look elsewhere to meet its full requirements. In the early 1990s, the IMF and the US government pressurized Haiti to reduce its tariffs on imports, and the tiny country capitulated. The US government then subsidized US farmers to the tune of $13 billion from 1995 on, in order that they could undercut domestic producers overseas. Haiti's domestic rice market (and with it, much of its agriculturally based economy) was decimated.[8]

US food producers won twice. First, Haiti became the second biggest importer of US rice on the planet. Second, the poverty and starvation caused by the collapse of Haiti's rice market proved to be a boon for US food aid. Each year, the US taxpayer gives $1.5 billion to US corporations to produce food for food aid, much of which would not be required without these market-wrecking policies.[9]

Investor-state disputes

Previous trade agreements have enabled corporations to sue countries, in a bid to strike down national laws and rights that impinge upon their ability to turn a profit. This has had very real impacts on domestic tax, public health and environmental policy across the globe.

In 2010, tobacco firm Philip Morris used 'investor-to-state dispute' rights created by the North American Free Trade Agreement to launch legal action against Uruguay at the World Trade Organization.[10] Uruguay had implemented a rule that 80 per cent of cigarette packaging must be devoted to health warnings. Philip Morris is seeking to claim $2 billion in damages from Uruguay for what it deems a trademark infringement – the remaining space being inadequate for their logo and branding. In 2012, Philip Morris launched parallel legal action against Australia, after parliament and the Supreme Court there backed similar moves to replace cigarette advertising with health warnings.[11]

Argentina has been sued more than any other country by the World Bank's International Centre for the Settlement of Investment Disputes – paying out over $1 billion in settlements to corporations.[12] During the height of its financial crisis after 2001, the government froze people's energy and water bills in a bid to halt the exponential rise in prices by the privatized utilities companies (a plan recently echoed by Labour leader Ed Miliband). The utilities companies responded by suing Argentina – and won. The law was struck down and Argentina was forced to pay hefty fines.

In 2009, three anti-mining campaigners (including a 32-year-old woman who was eight months pregnant) were murdered for their role opposing the creation of the Eldorado Gold Mine by the Pacific Rim Mining Corporation, in El Salvador.[13] Despite this enormous sacrifice and intimidation, the campaign grew and the local communities of Cabañas convinced the government that granting the application would pollute public water supplies and cause unacceptable environmental damage; plans for the mine were rejected. Pacific Rim Mining Corporation set out to use the Central America Free Trade Agreement (CAFTA) to sue the El Salvadorian government for $77 million.[14] The World Bank decided CAFTA was not the appropriate means by which to sue the government of El Salvador and gave Pacific Rim useful instructions on alternative avenues. In April 2013, Pacific Rim's US subsidiary filed claims of $315 million at the World Bank's International Centre for the Settlement of Investment Disputes.

Corporations will actively exploit the increased rights in TPP and TTIP to extend their own interests – maximizing profits. The public interest will be subordinated.

The corporate takeover

Tax evasion costs Europe one trillion euros each year – this is more than the combined spending on health, and four times the total spending on education.[15] TTIP claims to be worth an estimated 119 billion euros a year.

Yet, while pan-EU agreements on ending tax evasion languish unresolved, TTIP, at just one tenth of the value, in return for handing swathes of national sovereignty over to corporations and faceless supranational bodies, will be concluded in just 18-24 months.

According to the UK Parliament's briefing paper, TTIP entered the third round of negotiations on 16 December 2013, with the aim of concluding 'well before the pressures of the 2016 US presidential election bear down'.[16]

All democratic barriers are being moved aside in order to support this goal. In the UK, the High Level Working Group may well be ceded powers from Downing Street enabling sections of the agreement to come into force before the UK parliament has ratified it. In the US, there are plans to invoke the President's 'Trade Promotion Authority' to make it impossible for Congress to amend or debate TPP.[17] A significant number of the world's 'democracies' are being railroaded into these undemocratic agreements by corporatized governments. Such agreements will suppress internet freedom, restrict civil liberties, decimate internal economies, stop developing countries distributing the lowest-cost drugs, imperil public healthcare, and hand corporations the right to overturn decisions made by democratic governments in the public interest.

Your democratic representative will not be able to see or amend these agreements before they become legally binding – while corporate lobbyists will not only be able to see them, but will have written them. That such an egregiously undemocratic circumstance exists, speaks volumes about the corporate control of so-called democratic governments. But these agreements complete the ambitions of the neoliberal project, from 1944 to today – to end social democracy, its institutions and its protections. To establish a world run by corporations, for corporations.

Conclusion

The inevitable endgame of neoliberalism is corporate fascism, and the de-civilization of our world. The only way out is to abandon capitalism, in all its forms.

Some would argue that capitalism is trade, or ownership of property, or profit. But capitalism is not any of these things. It is an ideological basis for *how* we do these things.

This misunderstanding plays greatly into the hands of the chief beneficiaries of the status quo. They are able to take what is actually a very short-lived ideology – 400 years for capitalism and a mere half-century for its neoliberal variant – to present it as 'how we have always done things', and to credit it for every human achievement since humans stood upright.

Some would argue that, because the technological revolution that brought us the smartphone, the computer and the internet happened in the context of neoliberalism, that neoliberalism equals progress. But even if that were true (and it is not), are smartphones, the computer and the internet what distinguish us as a civilization? I would argue, no. Citizens of Bangladesh, Sudan and the Democratic Republic of Congo have smartphones, computers and the internet. They are still fighting for civilization.

What really distinguishes a civilization is the ability of people to access the benefits of that civilization. As has been shown in this book, those things that distinguish us as a civilization – human rights, a work-life balance, open and balanced justice, wages that meet the cost of living, access to a quality education, a welfare state, decent and affordable homes, labour laws that prevent exploitation of children and adults – all these things were not the result of capitalism. They were won *from* capitalism, by movements for social democracy, and only very recently. What neoliberalism has achieved is to reframe the ideology of capitalism to bulldoze those pillars of civilization. Neoliberalism has enabled an ever-widening wealth gap, which has handed economic and political power to a few incredibly wealthy individuals, institutions and corporations – and they are using that power to implement corporate fascism, as defined by US President Franklin Roosevelt. A reminder of that quote again:

'The liberty of a democracy is not safe if the people tolerate the growth of private power to a point where it becomes stronger than the democratic state itself. That in its essence is fascism: ownership of government by an individual, by a group, or any controlling private power.'

And at the other end of the wealth gap lie poverty and destitution. Those subject to poverty and destitution are no longer gifted with the benefits of civilization.

In 1914, Robert Tressell's landmark novel *The Ragged Trousered Philanthropists* was published. To this day, no other fiction title has so thoroughly captured the utter insanity of capitalism. At one point in the story, Owen, a character representing the voice of reason, states the following:

'What I call poverty is when people are not able to secure for themselves all the benefits of civilization; the necessaries, comforts, pleasures and refinements of life, leisure, books, theatres, pictures, music, holidays, travel, good and beautiful homes, good clothes, good and pleasant food.'

Neoliberalism's Zombie Economy created this poverty

by sucking value and wealth away from the majority and funnelling it to an élite minority. This puts a barrier between people and the benefits of a civilization that we all, and generations before us, participated in creating. As ever more value and wealth is removed, the result is destitution. Destitution is when the barrier to the benefits of civilization becomes insurmountable.

What use is the idea of a smartphone, a computer or the internet when you cannot afford to eat, to access medical developments that would treat your illness, to keep a roof over your head?

That is why this system, which allows for the constant expansion of poverty and destitution, has to be replaced. That is why we need to think systemically about transforming our world. Opposing Austerity while supporting capitalism is as futile as pouring water on a fire with one hand and petrol with the other.

Capitalism was a revolutionary idea 400 years ago. Neoliberalism was the opportunity to pretend that capitalism was something more than smash and grab, colonialism and empire. But inventions of neoliberalism such as Structural Adjustment, Austerity, and the ever-increasing dominance of corporate power to the point that it supersedes democratic power, are leading to the effective de-civilizing of our world, by barring an ever-increasing pool of people from access to those things that we consider the hallmarks of civilization.

Many do not see the systemic nature of this shift. Even many of those railing against the iniquities caused by this economic system are unable to see how or why these are systemic inevitabilities. If I took a step off the edge of a cliff, it is a physical certainty that my body would fall until it hit the ground. If a country implements neoliberalism, it is an economic certainty that inequality will increase. This is, quite simply, how the system works. So it is in the interests of those privileged few who reap maximum benefit from the system to avoid the majority from coming to that same conclusion – to keep them blissfully unaware that their disenfranchisement is both intentional and inevitable.

This is why politicians and large sections of the media, also corrupted by the system, spend their time inculcating in people the belief that too many immigrants, too many scroungers, a bloated public-sector bureaucracy, or any number of other scapegoats are to blame for the inherent failings of neoliberalism. They even go so far as to argue that the mythical properties of neoliberalism will actually cure these ills.

French poet Charles Baudelaire once wrote *'La plus belle des ruses du diable est de vous persuader qu'il n'existe pas'* – the devil's finest trick is to persuade you that he does not exist. This is the trick pulled by the neoliberal project. Convince billions of people that there is no plan; that we live in a post-ideological world; that there is a free market; that the trickle-down effect means that the best way of increasing the wealth of the poor is to increase the wealth of the rich. This is an absurdity. It flies in the face of all evidence to the contrary. It is propaganda, a fairy tale told to children.

If we take the myth of the 'free market' as an example: there never has been and never will be a capitalist free-market economy – and here is why.

Capitalism is meant to pivot around the free market. The theory goes that if only the market were rid of government meddling (regulation) then true competition would reign, with corporations battling it out to provide their goods and services to rational, all-knowing consumers. This, according to devotees of the idea, would provide stable and accurate prices and quality for goods and services as competition took effect via supply, demand and pricing. Corporations that provided a good or service which was not wanted, was above the market price or below the market quality demanded by the rational consumer in this open, free market would simply fail, while those that met demand would win. The success or failure of a company would be directly proportional to its ability to meet the needs of its customers.

Some might argue that recent failures assigned to capitalism – the bankers' bailout, the corporatization of government, the decline in social mobility – have occurred because we do not have **real** capitalism as outlined above. They might argue that we are in fact in a post-capitalist, state capitalist or fascist state. There are valid arguments in favour of all these possibilities. But whatever state we are in, it is as a direct and inevitable result of capitalism. These outcomes are not aberrations, but natural and logical given the reward mechanisms of the system itself.

While arguments in favour of inviting private interests into the public services rest on the idea of competition, corporations themselves are rabidly anti-competition. If a McDonald's opens opposite a Burger King, Burger King isn't over the moon that the capitalist theory of competition is being exercised, it is figuring out how to kill the opposition. The argument goes that the consumer is the ultimate beneficiary of this struggle, as the consumer will be tempted by lower prices and better-quality goods to win them over.

These arguments overlook some key issues. They ignore that it makes sense for the corporation to seek out a monopoly – a monopoly gained via the marketplace would in practice be no different from a socialized monopoly, except that any notion of democratic accountability would be removed.

They also fail to consider that the consumer is not solely a consumer but also a member of society and so may well be impacted by the competition in more than one way (in other words, they might benefit from a price cut as a consumer, but lose their job as a result of the bigger corporation pushing their own employer out of the market).

Consider the 'free market' policies started under the Thatcher and Reagan governments in the 1980s US and UK, and continued ever since by governments on both sides of the water. This might logically have been expected to result in a dramatic rise in competition, ending monopolies and ushering in a new era of dynamic, consumer-responsive businesses vying for attention.

Let us take food as a case study in considering whether this has actually come about. In 1990, only 10-20 per cent of global food retail was delivered by supermarkets.[18] Today, that figure has soared to 50-60 per cent. That is, over half of all food sold in the world is sold through supermarkets.

The UK has lost 90 per cent of its specialist food retailers – that is butchers, bakers and fishmongers – since the 1950s. In Britain today, 97 per cent of food purchased is bought in supermarkets, with only four corporations making up 76 per cent of those sales. In the US, 72 per cent of food is purchased in supermarkets.[19] As these figures continue on their upward trend, we can see that monopolies are being created in food production.

The rise of the supermarket since the 1950s has meant that the percentage of the US household budget spent on food has dropped from 32 per cent to 7 per cent.[20] In the UK, the proportion spent on food has dropped from 33 per cent to 15 per cent.[21] Proponents of capitalism would look at these statistics and argue: 'look, it worked'.

But, with supermarkets making record profits, and household food budgets down, who is paying the price for our food? The answer is: food producers and the environment. In Brazil, more than 75,000 farmers have been delisted by the big supermarkets. Thailand's top supermarket chain has carved its supplier list from 250 to just 10. The tiny country of Lesotho has actually all but killed off its domestic farming industry, with 99 per cent of its food purchased through supermarkets utilizing foreign agribusiness.[22]

Seventy years ago, there were nearly seven million American farmers; today there are two million. Between 1987 and 1992 the US lost 32,500 farms a year and now 75 per cent of US produce comes from just 50,000 farming operations.[23]

Family farming and smallholding have been the big victims of the supermarkets all over the world. This means farmers in developing countries have been exploited, and consumers in developed countries have become so far removed from their food chain that they could not tell the difference between beef and horse.

The inflation of food prices in recent years has been masked not only by supermarkets pressurising food producers to ever decreasing incomes and unsustainable farming practices, but the makeup of our food is being diluted... in short, the price might stay the same but we are getting less for our money. The 2013 horse-meat scandal is just one example of this.

So, when it comes to food, the encouragement of market forces has seen a few corporations rise to dominate, setting their own prices and leading to negative social impacts. While some consumers might see a fall in the price of the food they are buying, they cannot be sure that they are comparing apples with apples and it may be that while they are benefiting as consumers, they are losing out as producers.

In fact, if we zoom out to what is happening in business overall, for the last three years the US has seen a consistent fall in the total number of businesses. US start-ups (new businesses) have fallen as a share of total businesses from 12 per cent to just 7 per cent.[24]

These patterns are reflected across developed economies globally. The market contains a decreasing number of businesses, fewer new businesses are being launched and the monopolies created are having a negative impact upon communities across the globe.

What keeps a free market free? As we have seen above, it is not in the interest of the corporation to maintain a free market. The corporation has no reason to apply any kind of ethics whatsoever. Adidas employs child and sweatshop labour in the Far East[25] because it is cheaper than employing people on a living wage, with decent terms and conditions – those benefits of civilization won for us from capitalism generations ago.

Historically the government, as the purported servant of the people, has been the enforcer of rules necessary to restrain the 'market' from behaviours which, while logical from the point of view of the corporation, lead to undesirable social outcomes.

However, the logic of the corporation is then to seek maximum influence over the regulator, with corporations using their vast wealth to buy influence in houses of parliament or government across the globe.

In the US, by 2011, the largest 30 corporations spent more that year on lobbying government than they spent on taxes.[26] Big Oil alone spent over $169 million on lobbying the US government in 2009. Between 1998 and 2008 (the year of the bailout) the US banking sector spent $3.4 billion lobbying for deregulation, reduced capital requirements and avoiding the regulation of derivatives (all of which caused the financial crisis).[27] When corporations aren't lobbying, they are simply gaining positions of power within government itself so as directly to redraft legislation to suit them.

In the UK, corporations with outstanding tax issues with the HMRC (the tax collector) are currently in working groups with the HMRC to redraft the very tax rules they are doing their best to avoid.[28] The largest accountancy firms are also using consultancy positions within government as tax policy advisors to market themselves to tax-evading corporations, which hire them to break the rules they helped to write.[29]

In the US, there appears to be a revolving door between Monsanto (controversial purveyor of genetically modified foods) and the food regulating agencies. Islam Siddiqui, vice-president of Monsanto-funded lobby group CropLife, is now a negotiator for the US trade representative on agriculture. Roger Beachy, former director of a Monsanto-funded plant science centre, has become the director of the National Institute of Food and Agriculture.[30] Michael Taylor, former vice president of Monsanto, is now the deputy commissioner of the Food and Drug Administration, the US's regulator in the sector.[31]

There is a major problem here. When corporations break the law, they are either not tried or are given a fine that comes nowhere near the profits reaped by breaking the law. Worse, corporations are buying the drafting of laws which make their unethical and damaging behaviour legal.

Corporations do not want any rules to stand in the way of making profit. Left unregulated, they would simply operate in ways that maximized their profits regardless of social outcomes. When we introduce a regulator, corporations seek to and succeed in compromising them. This is natural and inevitable if they are left to their own devices – which is precisely why they need to be controlled.

The neoliberal phase of capitalism is a project which, if it is permitted to continue, will subjugate the public interest to the corporate interest. It has already subverted democracy and state power in the name of corporate power in many countries across the world, and in the last 30 years we have witnessed an escalation in this process, and an expansion of it to the 'developed world'. The horrors of austerity we have witnessed to date are mere trifles compared with the future that awaits us if we continue down this road to corporate fascism.

Ultimately, it all comes down to the question: what kind of future do we want?

Those generations of the early 20th century bequeathed us a welfare state including an NHS, a free state education for every child up to the age of 18, sickness and unemployment benefits, pensions, and high-quality, low-cost social housing.

But what will we leave behind for future generations? A society in which people are working longer, for lower wages, to receive a lower pension, only to die racking up exorbitant debts in a substandard care home… while those who could and should be caring for them are caught up on the same hamster wheel.

This is the future we are creating every time we choose to submit to and tolerate the latest neoliberal initiative, rather than to object to and oppose it.

Those who say that we cannot or will not win this struggle do an enormous injustice to the generations who brought us social democracy in the first place. They faced excruciating circumstances and overcame them through persistence and solidarity. This is all that is missing today. And it is not some gene that today's generations are sadly lacking. It is a forgotten skill that needs to be relearned. We need to do so – and fast. While many remain largely oblivious of the fact, a future is being written for them that is far from that post-War promise that brought us so much, so fast, that we forgot we earned it.

What solving the crisis might look like

The purpose of this book is not to present solutions in detail. The reason I devoted an entire book to identifying and characterizing our problems is – no-one wants a solution for a problem that doesn't exist to them. The lack of economic and political education in our society has created a population that struggles to ask the necessary questions.

I have attempted to plot a path through the timeline of events – from 1944 in Bretton Woods through to today – and to explain how these events, policies, agreements and decisions created the world we live in. At this stage, it should be clear to the reader that Austerity is neither temporary nor necessary, and that it will not bring about any kind of economic progress that will benefit the poorer 99 per cent of the population. Knowing this, people should be anxiously looking for an escape route.

How we find that escape route will be the subject of my next book. But there are a few things that could be done right now, to shore us up temporarily while we create a workable and sustainable economy.

Break up the banks

- Break up the big banks into many smaller ones that could fail in future without devastating the wider economy.
- Make it illegal for a bank to be both a retail bank and an investment bank.
- Hold individuals who are responsible for the financial crisis accountable in a court of law, sending a clear signal that people will not be allowed to profit by destroying their companies and the wider economy.

This was what the UK government publicly committed to ahead of the Vickers Report. But the proposals were watered down to such an extent that they will not reduce the banking sector as a proportion of GDP, will not separate casino banking from retail banking, and will not outlaw derivatives trading.

Increase wages

Introduce legislation increasing the minimum wage of £6.31 per hour, to the living wage of £7.65 an hour (£8.80 in London). Prosecute any employer that pays any member of staff less than this amount.

While neoliberal economists argue that this would have a detrimental impact on the economy, research by the National Institute for Economic and Social Research for the Resolution Foundation found these dangers to be overestimated. They found that adopting the living wage would see just a 0.5-percent aggregate reduction in labour demand – which would be vastly outweighed by the benefits. As one of Britain's leading business and economics commentators and assistant editor of the *Daily Telegraph* Jeremy Warner (a proud capitalist) wrote in April 2013:

'Substantially raising the minimum wage immediately addresses two major economic anomalies. One is the now perverse growth in corporate profits and cash accumulation. Rather than being recycled into the economy, which is what happens in normal times, corporate profits are being hoarded, further eating into demand. In the US, corporate profits as a proportion of GDP are at a record high. Wages, by contrast, are at a post-War low... I don't lightly dismiss the right to make or even hoard profits, but things are getting seriously out of kilter. This is not the way capitalism is supposed to work, where wealth accumulation gets shared through trickle-down effects. The division of spoils has reached a level which, if unaddressed, threatens to be dangerously destabilizing, socially and politically.

'The other issue concerns the use of means-tested tax credits to top up people's takehome pay. That the taxpayer should be subsidizing low-paid work in this way is totally absurd and should be ended as soon as possible. Indeed, it explains quite a lot of Britain's economic predicament – with excessive levels of household borrowing and now fast-growing government debt. Debt has become a substitute for income.'[32]

Even within the warped logic of capitalism, raising the minimum wage to the level of a living wage makes sense. It would support the reduction of consumer debt, would increase consumer spending, and would decrease income inequality.

Control the cost of living

Introduce price control measures on items on the UK Essentials Index (except tobacco and alcohol), namely:

- Gas and electricity
- Vehicle and tax insurance
- Petrol and oil
- Water and related charges
- Transport fares
- Home insurance
- Council tax and rates
- Food and rent.

Reducing the cost of the essentials would mean the consumer's budget has more room to accommodate saving and pension contributions. This would take the pressure off public finances in the short and medium term.

Abandon neoclassical economics

The dominance of this model is dangerous. When 'economists' are produced on panel shows, news interviews and government working groups, they are always neoclassical economists. Whether they are Keynesians or Friedmanites, they share certain fundamental presumptions. Such economists use models to forecast economic performance that do not even include debt, money or time as factors.[33] They contributed to the financial crisis by endorsing the behaviour of the financial services industry and of the governments that deregulated that industry. They not only failed to foresee the financial crisis, but actually said that it was an impossibility.[34] To continue to seek answers from this community when they have so clearly been proven wrong, is utter folly.

Economics professor Steve Keen suggests that we pretend for a moment that the financial collapse was a physical collapse.

If in 2008, all suspension bridges in the world collapsed, and we found that the architecture of suspension bridges meant they would inevitably collapse every 30 years, creating massive devastation, wouldn't we want to opt for a better design for our bridges? And wouldn't we want to ensure that those engineers who designed the bridges and told us they were safe, were held to account?

Our reaction to the financial crisis, in contrast, was to compensate its engineers with public money and to dismiss its critics as radicals. The government, meanwhile, continued actively replacing safer, alternatively designed bridges with suspension bridges.

These economists must go, and investment should be made through universities and research councils to develop the newer schools of economics which embrace the breakthroughs in mathematics and physics to develop more robust models with which to predict outcomes.

Last word

Now these changes would not enable the kind of paradigm shift we need to deliver an equitable socio-economic model, but they would at least give us a chance of organizing ourselves better while we develop our alternatives. If your appetite has been whetted, and you are eager to know more about the myriad options available to us to organize, trade and co-exist – I will explore these in detail in my next book.

In the meantime, keep learning, keep protesting and keep thinking creatively about solutions to our problems. I don't campaign for change because the system or the individuals within it are evil. I campaign because I believe human beings are infinitely capable and ingenious. When we co-operate, we become greater than the sum of our parts. For me it is not a matter of if we replace this system, it is when, and I want this to be as soon as possible so that we end the avoidable and unnecessary iniquities that this book has described. You may have been working at the project of change your whole life, or you may have just started – or you may have been afraid or unwilling to start before now. Wherever you are in that spectrum, I acknowledge you for choosing to read this book and to absorb its contents.

We need to understand it deep in our bones that the cavalry is not coming. We ourselves are the cavalry. Only our newly emerging people's campaigns and institutions can resolve the crisis, because the existing institutions not only created it, but exist to serve it.

1 *Independent*, 14 Nov 2013, nin.tl/1AQo33V **2** Wikileaks, nin.tl/1sXxMoB **3** Corporate Europe Observatory, nin.tl/1AQplXm **4** High-level Working Group nin.tl/1sXB4lt & Parliament nin.tl/1sXBDCc **5** BBC news, 4 Jul 2012, nin.tl/1AQr8Bc **6** *Business Insider*, nin.tl/1sXEuer & nin.tl/1AQswnk **7** Commons Library, nin.tl/1sXBDCc **8** *Global Post*, 12 Apr 2012, nin.tl/1sXIFXt **9** Centre for Research on Globalization, nin.tl/1AQu298 **10** Mercopress, 19 Mar 2012, nin.tl/1sXTj0v **11** *Guardian*, 27 Jun 2011, nin.tl/1sXUX20 **12** Mercopress, 19 Oct 2010, nin.tl/1AQAtcg **13** Council of Canadians, 30 Dec 2009, nin.tl/1sXY3Ds **14** Council of Canadians, 2 Apr 2013, nin.tl/1AQBCk3 **15** *Huffington Post*, 5 Jun 2013, nin.tl/1sY0wxq **16** UK Parliament briefing paper, nin.tl/1sXBDCc **17** *Independent*, 14 Nov 2013, nin.tl/1AQo33V **18** Peter Wilby, *Guardian* comment is free, nin.tl/1sY767c **19** PRWeb, 16 Sep 2012, nin.tl/1wlVB9s **20** Investopedia, nin.tl/1sY8oz8 **21** BBC news, 28 Jan 2008, nin.tl/1wlW2R3 **22** http://www.endinghunger.org **23** Kerr Center, nin.tl/1wlWBKT **24** Reuters, 26 Jun 2012, nin.tl/1sYcreT & nin.tl/1wlWQW8 **25** BBC news, 7 Jun 2012, nin.tl/1sYdJGw **26** *Daily Finance*, 13 Dec 2011, nin.tl/1wlXdzY **27** *New Internationalist*, Oct 2011, nin.tl/1sYgN5J **28** Parliament.uk, nin.tl/1wlXSkZ **29** Reuters, 31 Jan 2013, nin.tl/1sYtL3c **30** *New Internationalist*, Oct 2011, nin.tl/1sYgN5J **31** *Natural News*, 25 Oct 2012, nin.tl/1wm0SxX **32** *Telegraph*, 2 Apr 2013, nin.tl/1sYvXYl **33** Steve Keen's Debtwatch, 24 Mar 2009, nin.tl/1wm1ovG **34** Kamran Mofid, nin.tl/1sYxgqx

About the New Internationalist

New Internationalist is an award-winning, independent media co-operative. Our aim is to inform, inspire and empower people to build a fairer, more sustainable planet.

We publish a global justice magazine and a range of books, both distributed worldwide. We have a vibrant online presence and run ethical online shops for our customers and other organizations.

❖ **Independent media:** we're free to tell it like it is – our only obligation is to our readers and the subjects we cover.

❖ **Fresh perspectives:** our in-depth reporting and analysis provide keen insights, alternative perspectives and positive solutions for today's critical global justice issues.

❖ **Global grassroots voices:** we actively seek out and work with grassroots writers, bloggers and activists across the globe, enabling unreported (and under-reported) stories to be heard.

newint.org